A Daily Word

FOR Boys

A 365-DAY DEVOTIONAL

BroadStreet
PUBLISHING

BroadStreet Kids
Savage, Minnesota, USA
BroadStreet Kids is an imprint of BroadStreet Publishing Group, LLC.
Broadstreetpublishing.com

A Daily Word for Boys

© 2023 by BroadStreet Publishing®

9781424565894
9781424565900 (eBook)

Devotional entries composed by Natasha Marcellus.

Typesetting and design by Garborg Design Works | garborgdesign.com
Editorial services by Carole Holdahl and by Michelle Winger | literallyprecise.com

Printed in China.

23   24   25   26   27   28   29   7   6   5   4   3   2   1

How can a young person

keep their life pure?

By living according

to your word.

PSALM 119:9 NIRV

Introduction

Living for God can be hard. You might have heard many different messages about what is right and wrong, and that can be very confusing. God's Word is full of truth and life, and it can lead you into making good decisions every day.

Spending time with God helps you to be a boy who is full of courage, kindness, and joy. Each devotion in this book begins with one word for the day. Think about this word as you read the connected Bible verse, devotion, and question. Remember the word as you go about your day and see if it changes the way you think about things.

Let Jesus bring light and peace to your heart as you listen to his wisdom. When other people see his light shining in you, they will want it too!

JANUARY

God is our refuge and strength,

always ready to help

in times of trouble.

PSALM 46:1 NLT

Purpose

In Christ we were chosen to be God's people. God had already chosen us to be his people, because that is what he wanted. And God is the One who makes everything agree with what he decides and wants. We are the first people who hoped in Christ. And we were chosen so that we would bring praise to God's glory.

EPHESIANS 1:11-12 ICB

Alex liked to dream. As he rode his bike along his driveway, he liked to imagine who he would be when he grew up. He imagined running into burning buildings as a firefighter or solving problems as an engineer. He imagined walking his dog and traveling to cool places. He liked to think about all the exciting things he would do with his life.

It is great to imagine what kind of life you will live. God has given you great dreams! But no matter what you do in your life, your most important purpose is to glorify God. You might grow up to be a father, a husband, a teacher, a pilot, or a business owner. No matter how you spend your time or what job you do, you are first and foremost a chosen son of God.

What are some ways you can honor God every day?

Decision

"If you refuse to serve the LORD,
then choose today whom you will serve.
But as for me and my family, we will serve the LORD."

JOSHUA 24:15 NLT

Cameron knew his friends weren't making good choices. His heart told him that he shouldn't follow along when they were being unkind to others or disobeying the rules. He knew he should stand up for what is right, but he was nervous and he didn't want to be alone or different from his friends.

Every day you are faced with choices. Even though doing the right thing can be scary, you are the only one who can control your actions. No matter what anyone else does, the choice to do the right thing is one hundred percent up to you. When you are nervous, ask God for strength and he will give you the courage to serve him in all you do.

When those around you do something you know is wrong, how can you honor God with your choices?

Respected

An overseer must be so good that people cannot rightly criticize him. He must have only one wife. He must have self-control and be wise. He must be respected by other people and must be ready to help people by accepting them into his home. He must be a good teacher. He must not drink too much wine, and he must not be a man who likes to fight. He must be gentle and peaceful. He must not love money.

1 TIMOTHY 3:2-3 ICB

Simon sat in church with his parents. He didn't feel like going to Sunday school that morning and so he was listening to the sermon instead. The pastor was talking about leadership and Simon thought that it was boring. Isn't leadership basically just telling people what to do? As the pastor talked more about it, Simon started to realize that maybe it's more complicated than that.

Leadership is a serious job. There are many areas in life where you can be a leader, but the Bible specifically talks about what it means to be a leader in the church. If that is something you want to do, you can look to the Word to see how you will need to live. God loves his children so much that he wants the people who teach them to be kind, qualified, and self-controlled. He doesn't want people to be hurt by harsh, proud leaders.

How does good leadership help the people being led?

Brave

"Here's what I've learned through it all:
Don't give up; don't be impatient;
be entwined as one with the Lord.
Be brave and courageous, and never lose hope.
Yes, keep on waiting—for he will never disappoint you!"

PSALM 27:14 TPT

Eric opened the door to the room where youth group was being held. As he stepped inside, he looked around and didn't recognize a single face. His family had recently moved to a new town and his mom thought it was important for him to make friends at church. They had prayed before she dropped him off, that he would be brave and courageous. His mom knew big groups made him nervous. As he looked across the room, he saw another boy wearing his favorite team's jersey. He took a deep breath and went to ask him about it.

God is on your side. He is with you all of the time and he knows exactly what you need. He doesn't command you to be brave and then leave you alone to figure it out. He says to be brave and courageous because he is always there to help. He will encourage you and strengthen you when you need it most.

Can you think of a time when God has encouraged you and helped you when you needed it?

Stay

"Remain in me, and I will remain in you.
No branch can produce fruit alone.
It must remain in the vine.
It is the same with you.
You cannot produce fruit alone.
You must remain in me."

JOHN 15:4 ICB

Jake didn't understand his homework. He hadn't paid attention during the instructions, and he didn't want to take the time to ask for help. Instead, he scribbled something down even though he knew it was wrong. The next day when they were going over the assignment, he wished he had taken the time to ask for help. It was simple and would have only taken him a few minutes.

You will always be better off when you ask for help. You aren't meant to live your life alone. This is true every day and with God. Stay close to him and he will take care of you. Spend time with him and you will produce good fruit. If you try to get through your life without him, it is like cutting yourself off from the best help you could ever be given.

Is there a problem in your life that you
have tried to tackle on your own?

Appropriate

Everyone enjoys giving great advice.
But how delightful it is
to say the right thing at the right time!
PROVERBS 15:23 TPT

Jason was talking with a group of his friends. He was trying to explain why Aaron, his brother who had Down's syndrome, spoke the way he did. He sounded different and his friends didn't understand. One boy made a rude comment while another talked about how much fun Aaron was to be around. He was joyful and observed things in a unique way. Later that day, Jason thought about his two friends and how their words were so opposite. One had taken the time to say something meaningful while the other had just spewed out what was on the tip of his tongue. Jason didn't want to spend time with someone who spoke so rudely.

What you say matters. Your words can either encourage or discourage someone and you are the only one who can control what comes out of your mouth. Try to be the kind of person who speaks carefully and says things that will lift others up. When you are careless with your words, you can tear people down and create lasting damage. Instead, bring life with what you say.

How can you practice controlling what you say?
Who can you lift up with your words today?

Faith

Faith means being sure of the things we hope for. And faith means knowing that something is real even if we do not see it.

HEBREWS 11:1 ICB

Trent knew God was real. He had learned about him his whole life but on some days, he just felt really far away. He was busy with school, sports, activities, and friends. Sometimes days went by when he didn't even think about God. He wasn't sure if he was doing a very good job at following Jesus.

Have you ever felt discouraged by your faith? It can be hard to think about God when he isn't right in front of you. This doesn't make you a bad Christian. God knew we would struggle. That's why he sent the Holy Spirit to guide us when he can't be directly with us. The more you walk with him, the stronger your faith will get. Just because you can't see something, doesn't mean it isn't real. Faith is like a muscle; when you use it even a little bit each day, it will become stronger. God is so proud of your desire to follow him!

How can you strengthen your faith a little bit today?

Character

God's people need to be very patient. They are the ones who
obey God's commands. And they remain faithful to Jesus.

REVELATION 14:12 NIRV

Orlando was having a difficult day. As he sat with his mom
before bedtime he listened closely as she encouraged him.
She shared that one day, everything would be perfect. She
said when Jesus returns he will make all things right and we
just need to wait patiently for him to come back. Orlando
couldn't even really understand what "perfect" meant but it
sounded great. He was excited about a day when he wouldn't
fight with his friends, or struggle to grasp a concept at
school. His mom's words lifted his spirits and he fell asleep
dreaming about what a perfect world would look like.

One day, Jesus will come back again. He will make all things
right and will wipe every tear from your eyes. As you wait
for him, let God help build your character. He can help you
to be patient and kind even when life is hard. Waiting is hard
but your patience will be rewarded one day.

How can you build your character
as you look forward to Jesus' return?

Excited

I'm asking the LORD for only one thing.
Here is what I want.
I want to live in the house of the LORD
all the days of my life.

PSALM 27:4 NIRV

Ryan's thoughts were occupied with beach days, lazy mornings, video games, and ice cream. He was barely halfway through the school year but all he could do was dream about summer. He couldn't wait for school to be out so he could enjoy summer vacation. With each week that went by, Ryan became more and more excited. He kept a list in his room of all of the things he wanted to do and when he got discouraged at school, he would think about all of the fun that was to come.

Have you ever wanted something so badly it's all you can think about? Maybe you were really excited about a vacation or someone you love was coming to visit. It's all you can think about, and it keeps you awake at night because you're so excited. Maybe you count down the days or you daydream about how great it will be. You tell everyone you know about it, and you can't help talking about it whenever you get a chance. This is how we are supposed to view God. We should be excited to be worship him and spend time with him.

When you think about God and all he has done,
do you feel excited?

Authority

You will know that God's power is very great for us who believe. That power is the same as the great strength God used to raise Christ from death and put him at his right side in heaven. God made Christ more important than all rulers, authorities, powers, and kings. Christ is more important than anything in this world or in the next world.

EPHESIANS 1:19-21 ICB

In history class Micah was learning about different governments around the world. They had been talking about the upcoming presidential election as well and Micah had a lot of questions. It seemed like everyone had a different opinion about how a country should be run. After dinner he asked his dad what he thought. He looked at Micah and explained that the leading of countries was in the hands of God. He explained that Jesus is the true King and he is more important than any government.

A lot will change in your lifetime. You will see leaders rise and fall. You will see countries at war, and you will see times of peace. No matter what happens or who is in charge, remember that Jesus is your true king. He is the real authority. Look to him for leadership and guidance. His power is greater than anyone else's no matter how powerful they may seem.

When the news of what's happening in the world seems overwhelming, how can you trust in the true King?

Empathy

Be joyful with those who are joyful.
Be sad with those who are sad.

ROMANS 12:15 NIRV

Elijah walked to the park from his house. When he got there, he saw a group of his friends playing basketball. He also noticed one of his friends, Finlay, sitting on the swings with a troubled look on his face. Elijah had done all of his homework and cleaned his room extra early so he could play basketball that afternoon. He really wanted to join the game. Instead, he walked over to the swings and asked Finlay how he was doing.

It's easy to ignore people who are hurting. It's easy to keep going about your day, pretending you didn't notice someone having a hard time. You can tell yourself you don't have time or it's not your business. This is not what the Bible tells us to do. God says to be sad with those who are sad. Even when you don't feel like it, it is important to reach out and to be supportive of someone who is going through something difficult.

Ask God to open your eyes to see those who are hurting. How can you reach out and support someone who is going through a hard time?

Empowered

"Thomas, now that you've seen me, you believe.
But there are those who have never seen me with their eyes
but have believed in me with their hearts,
and they will be blessed even more!"

JOHN 20:29 TPT

Ethan sometimes imagined what it would be like to have Jesus alive right now. It would be so great if he could be here right now, performing miracles and teaching us how to love God. He could fix so many problems! It would be so much easier to be a Christian if he could just sit face-to-face with Jesus.

It does seem tempting to think about how lucky the disciples who walked with Jesus were. They could hear his voice, ask him questions, and see his face when he spoke. But did you know that because you have not seen Jesus, you will be even more blessed? The Bible says that because you have followed him with just the faith in your heart, you will be rewarded even more. You have been empowered to follow Jesus by the grace of God. God knows how hard it is to have faith in something you cannot see, and he is very proud of you.

Even though you can't see Jesus, what can you do
to strengthen your faith today?

Sure

Jesus said to her, "I am the resurrection and the life. Anyone who believes in me will live, even if they die. And whoever lives by believing in me will never die. Do you believe this?"

JOHN 11:25-26 NIRV

Hudson grew up going to church every week. He was part of the youth group and most of his friends believed in God. Even though he was surrounded by godly people, he sometimes felt like maybe he wasn't a good enough Christian. He felt unsure of his relationship with God and thought maybe he wasn't doing a good enough job.

It is normal to sometimes doubt your relationship with God. When this happens, turn to what the Bible says. It is clear in the book of John that those who believe in Jesus, the Son of God, who was raised from the dead, will never die. You can find security in that truth. Nothing else matters. All of your doubts can be answered by Jesus assuring you that he is the reason you are saved, not because of anything you have done.

When you doubt your relationship with God, how can you remember the truth of what Jesus said?

Dependable

A friend is always loyal,
and a brother is born to help in time of need.

PROVERBS 17:17 NLT

Johan was having a rough day. His parents were stressed out about something, and he was struggling with his math homework. He put his head down on his desk and sighed. Just then Brandon, who sat next to him, reached over and passed him a note. Johan opened it and laughed at the funny drawing Brandon had done. He looked at his friend and smiled. He was thankful to have Brandon in his life.

There is nothing better than a good friend. When you are feeling down, a kind friend makes all the difference. The Bible says that a friend is always loyal, and a brother helps in times of need. This is the kind of friend you should strive to be. Pay attention to those around you and take notice when there are opportunities to help others.

How can you practice being a good friend today?

Content

I know how to live when I am poor. And I know how to live
when I have plenty. I have learned the secret of being happy
at any time in everything that happens. I have learned
to be happy when I have all that I need and when I
do not have the things I need.

PHILIPPIANS 4:12 ICB

Oliver sat on the bus quietly. He listened to the other kids
talking about what they were going to do over summer
vacation. One friend was going to California to visit their
grandparents. Someone else was taking a family vacation
to Florida while another classmate had a season pass to
the water park. Everyone seemed to have something really
exciting planned. Oliver thought about hanging out in his
backyard with his brother and he felt disappointed. It was
hard to be happy about summer break when it looked like it
would be so boring.

When you start comparing yourself to others, you can
quickly feel like your life isn't good enough. There will always
be someone who is doing something more exciting or has
something you want. Finding contentment means being
satisfied with what you have already been given. When you
are content, jealousy has no way of creeping in. Focus on the
good things you have instead of all you think you are missing.

How can you practice being content?

Generous

Anyone who is kind to poor people lends to the LORD.
God will reward them for what they have done.

PROVERBS 19:17 NIRV

Jude sat in the car at the gas station. His dad was outside pumping gas and Jude was anxiously waiting for them to get going. His first soccer game of the season was tonight, and he didn't want to be late. While he watched his dad, eager for him to get in the car, he saw him walk back inside. He came out with a bag of snacks and headed to the side of the building. Jude watched curiously as his dad handed the bag and a twenty-dollar bill to a man sitting against the side of the building. When he got back in the car, he explained there is always time to be kind, especially when you have more than you need.

There is always room to be generous. A couple of dollars might not be important to you but for someone else, it could show them they are seen and loved. When you are generous with what you have, whether it's a little or a lot, you show other people how God feels about them.

How can you be generous and kind to those around you in need? Do you have to have money to be generous?

Grace

God continues to give us more grace. That's why Scripture
says, "God opposes those who are proud.
But he gives grace to those who are humble."

JAMES 4:6 NIRV

Josh stomped around the house. He was running out of
time before they needed to leave, and he couldn't find any
socks. He stomped down the stairs to the laundry room, he
stomped back up to his room, and he stomped over to the
bathroom hoping to find some laying around. He looked
under his bed, and he looked behind the closet door, all the
while exclaiming how frustrated he was. When he finally
asked his mom for help, she handed him a pair of socks. "I
did the laundry last night; your socks are all in your drawer.
Next time, just ask."

Missing socks might seem like a silly example, but the truth
is there are lots of times in life when we would be better
off by just asking for help. When you ask for help, you are
admitting you cannot do it alone. This is called humility.
God promises to always help those who are humble. He
cannot help someone who is prideful because they don't
even realize they need help.

Is there an area of your life you have
been struggling through on your own?
In what ways can you ask for help?

Pride

"Don't continue bragging.
Don't speak proud words.
The Lord is a God who knows everything.
He judges what people do."

1 SAMUEL 2:3 NIV

Wyatt got an A on his math test. He was so proud of himself. He raced home to tell his family all about it. When he got there, his sister was crying. She was sitting at the kitchen table with their mom, explaining how her science presentation didn't go well and how upset she was because she'd worked so hard on it. Wyatt folded up his math test and put it into his backpack. He walked over to his sister and tried to encourage her instead. Her sadness seemed more important than his victory at the moment. Later, when he showed his mom his test, she smiled at him. She knew how happy he was about his test, and she was proud of him for thinking of his sister's feelings. Wyatt didn't let pride get in the way of loving others.

There is no need to brag or speak proudly at the expense of others. God knows all you have done, and he will be faithful to reward you. You don't have to seek after your own rewards because he is a good Father who sees all you do.

Have you been elevating yourself above others?
How can you turn proud words into humble words?

Legacy

We will not hide these truths from our children;
we will tell the next generation
about the glorious deeds of the LORD,
about his power and his mighty wonders.

PSALM 78:4 NLT

Crosby sat at a picnic table at his grandparents' farm.
His family was gathered there for their big annual family
reunion. He even had a great-grandma who was still able
to come. At ninety-five, she was the oldest person there.
His cousin was only a few weeks old and was being passed
around by doting aunts and uncles. His great grandma was
telling stories about her childhood and Crosby couldn't
believe how different the world was now from how it was
when she was growing up. He looked around and thought
about how so many people in his family followed Jesus. They
were taught by their parents, who learned from their parents.

God loves families. He loves it when parents teach their
children about who he is. Maybe you didn't learn about God
from your mom or dad but whoever gave you this book
was passing down truth to you because they love you. They
declared to you that God is good, and you can do the same for
the next generation. As we share God's love his kingdom grows.

What have you learned about God from someone
older than you? What can you teach to someone else?

Leader

Choose some capable men from among the people. Choose men who respect God and who can be trusted. They will not change their decisions for money. Make these men officers over groups of 1,000, 100, 50 and 10 people.

EXODUS 18:21 ICB

Kai sat in class as the teacher sorted everyone into groups for a science project. He really wanted to be the leader in his group. He didn't like being told what to do and so he figured leading the group would take care of that. By the end of the project, he wasn't so sure his plan had worked. He had gotten frustrated with all of the questions, felt like he needed to fix everyone's problems, and ended up doing more of the work than seemed fair. Being a leader was a lot harder than he imagined.

The Bible is full of descriptions of good and bad leaders. Being in front of other people, teaching them and guiding them, is something God takes seriously. He calls leaders to be honest, upright, and capable. He says they should respect God and not be tempted by power or money.

It is good to aspire to leadership, but it should be taken seriously. How can God prepare your heart to be a leader who is responsible, trustworthy, and kind?

Thoughtful

We who are strong must be considerate of those who are
sensitive about things like this. We must not just please
ourselves. We should help others do what is right
and build them up in the Lord. For even Christ
didn't live to please himself.

ROMANS 15:1-3 NLT

Caleb loved playing board games with his family. One
afternoon he was playing a game with his sister. He was off
to a strong start and could feel a whole string of competitive
jabs on the tip of his tongue. His sister wasn't doing well,
and he knew if he played his cards right, he would quickly
win. Just as he was about to start talking about his victory,
he noticed her face. She looked frustrated and upset. She
couldn't figure out what to do next. Instead of gloating, he
changed his approach and asked her if she needed help. She
smiled and he thought about how different her reaction
would have been if he'd joked around like he was planning.

Sometimes you'll find yourself in situations like Caleb's.
There is nothing wrong with some competitive joking but if
you know it will hurt someone else, then you should instead
do whatever will lift them up. Sometimes the right thing is
simply what is best for someone else.

How can you practice thinking about
others before yourself?

Healthy

Training the body has some value.
But being godly has value in every way.
It promises help for the life you are now living
and the life to come.

1 TIMOTHY 4:8 NIRV

One Sunday at church, Maddox's teacher mentioned
spiritual strength. Maddox listened carefully because he had
never heard that phrase before. He knew it was important
to keep his mind healthy. That's why he loved reading and
learning new things. He knew it was important to keep
his body healthy. That's why he loved playing sports and
running around outside. But he had never heard that he
needed to be spiritually healthy. He wasn't even really sure
what that meant.

Being spiritually healthy is a lot like keeping your mind
and body healthy. You can exercise godliness and become
stronger. When you practice walking in godliness it will
benefit every area of your life. You can read the Bible, talk to
God in prayer, or even write down what you know about God.

How can you become spiritually stronger today
than you were yesterday?

Pleasant

The LORD is all I need.
He takes care of me.
My share in life has been pleasant;
my part has been beautiful.

PSALM 16:5-6 NCV

Jonas sat on the couch on a Thursday evening. He looked around and observed his family for a minute. His sister was finishing her homework at the dining room table. His dad was outside grilling dinner. His mom was on her way home from work and his grandma would be there soon to join them for dinner. He knew he was blessed to have a loving family and a safe, warm home. They drove him nuts a lot of the time, but they really were his favorite people in the whole world.

If you take a moment to think about it, you'll be able to see the ways God has blessed you. He has placed people, things, and memories in your life to bring you joy. He takes good care of his children. He knows what you need, and he is happy to provide you with it. Every good gift you have, big or small, is from him.

What has God given you today that has
made your life more pleasant or beautiful?

Motivated

Everything a person does might seem pure to them.
But the LORD knows why they do what they do.

PROVERBS 16:2 NIRV

Aiden was arguing with his sister. They were fighting over
whether or not she meant to run into him in the kitchen. She
had knocked his drink out of his hand and cleaning up the
mess made him angry. "You meant to do that!" he shouted.
Back and forth they went, each accusing the other and getting
more frustrated with each word. Once the mess was cleaned
up and they had both calmed down, Aiden apologized to her.
"I'm sorry I accused you of hurting me on purpose."

It's really easy to make judgements about why other people
act the way they do. It's easy to think you have the answers
to every situation or you are the only one who sees it clearly.
The truth is only God can see into the hearts of people.
He is the only one who knows our motives and our truest
thoughts. When you make assumptions, you take the other
person's voice away from them. Instead, try asking questions.
Ask God to help you see others the way he sees them.

When you let God be the one to look at someone's
heart, how does that change how you feel
in a difficult situation?

Mindful

Why is man important to you?
Why do you take care of human beings?

PSALM 8:4 ICB

Jesse walked through the park and quickly stopped when he heard a tiny squeak. He looked down and there at his feet was a baby bird. He had almost stepped on it. He looked up and saw a nest on a nearby branch. It must have fallen or was still learning to fly. He placed it carefully by the trunk of the tree where he knew it wouldn't get stepped on. Even though he was much bigger than the bird, and he could have ignored it, he did his best to keep it safe.

If Jesse noticed a tiny little bird and was willing to move it to safety, can you imagine how God feels about you? He is mindful of you. This means he thinks about you. You are always on his mind. He created you and he is the one who cares for you. As you turn to him, he will protect you and lead you.

How does knowing that God is mindful of you
change how you go about your day?

Moral

People shouted at him and made fun of him. But he didn't do the same thing back to them. When he suffered, he didn't say he would make them suffer. Instead, he trusted in the God who judges fairly.

1 PETER 2:23 NIRV

Thomas read 1 Peter 2:23 in his Bible. When he read it, he felt sad because he knew he hadn't followed Jesus' example. When he was upset, he really wanted other people to be upset. In the past, when someone said something, he didn't like he would think really hard and throw back the worst insult he could think of. When reading his Bible, he realized that's not how Jesus lived. If Jesus could trust in God during the worst time of his life, then Thomas could try to as well.

Jesus is sometimes called the Suffering Servant. He loved others completely even when they were horrible to him. This is the example we are supposed to follow. It's not easy, but with God's help, you can love others in that way. You can be a peacemaker; you can be full of kindness even when other people aren't.

Is there someone in particular you fight with most often, maybe a sibling or someone at school you don't get along with? How can you show them kindness instead?

Positive

A cheerful heart makes you healthy.
But a broken spirit dries you up.

PROVERBS 17:22 NIRV

Josiah walked through the kitchen and grabbed a snack off the counter. As he walked away, he read the sign above the kitchen sink. It was Proverbs 17:22 written in pretty cursive letters. His mom loved that verse, and he could see how it was true in her life. Things weren't always easy for his family but his mom had joy and strived to make their home a cheerful place. She was loving and kind and even when something difficult happened, she trusted that God's guidance was better than being anxious. Josiah was thankful for an example of how to lean on the Lord in good times and in bad times.

God doesn't ask you to be happy and smiley all of the time. He knows life can be hard and some days it is more difficult to be joyful. He is with you on those days he and he will comfort you when life is hard. He is the one who can fix your broken spirit. He is the one who can make your heart cheerful. This doesn't mean you will always feel happy, but it does mean when hard things happen, you will have the perseverance to get through them.

God is the only one who can turn your sadness into joy. When you're having a bad day, where do you turn?

Mature

We will speak the truth with love. We will grow up in every
way to be like Christ, who is the head. The whole body
depends on Christ. And all the parts of the body are joined
and held together. Each part of the body does its own work.
And this makes the whole body grow and be strong with love.

EPHESIANS 4:15-16 ICB

David couldn't wait to be older. He was so tired of being told
what to do. Having some freedom just seemed like the best
thing he could imagine. He couldn't wait to be on his own,
making his own decisions. He didn't think he needed anyone
else to help him.

As you get older, you might think you will grow more and
more independent. You might long for a time when you can
do things on your own and have some freedom. The truth is,
we all need each other. As your responsibility grows, you'll
actually need the people around you even more. We are
supposed to support each other and teach each other with
love and kindness no matter how old you get. The ability
to do what you've been created to do while supporting and
loving those around you is a mark of true maturity. You are
part of the body of Christ and are greatly needed.

How can you support part of the body of Christ today?
Who can you encourage?

Patient

Patient endurance is what you need now,
so that you will continue to do God's will.
Then you will receive all that he has promised.

HEBREWS 10:36 NLT

Daniel was excited about high school, he was excited about
driving his own car, and he was excited about seeing what it
would be like to be an adult. He felt like those days couldn't
come fast enough. He didn't want to be a kid anymore. He
wished he could just skip some steps and get to the fun stuff.

In life, as well as in your relationship with God, skipping
the steps you don't like might seem tempting. It's easy to
think another season or time will be better than where you
are right now. The truth is, God knows all of your days. He
knows exactly what your life will look like and exactly what
you need. Building patient endurance is better than rushing.
If you try to rush through your life, you will miss some of
what God has for you right now.

How can you be patient with where you are right now
instead of wishing for the next big thing?

Meaningful

Everything you speak to me is like joyous treasure,
filling my life with gladness.

PSALM 119:111 TPT

Hunter's family was on vacation. They were spending a week at the beach, and he was loving it. He sat on his towel reading a comic book his dad had bought him for the trip. As he looked up, he saw his little brother racing through the sand. Suddenly, he dropped to his knees and dug his hands into ground. He smiled joyously and scooped up a treasure to add to his bucket. He was so delighted by each shell he found that Hunter couldn't help but smile along with him.

The Word of God is a lot like those seashells on the beach and we can be just like Hunter's brother. Every single thing God has said to you is meaningful and valuable. You can search God's Word with joyous anticipation just like a child searching for treasures on the beach. His Word is precious and full of goodness. If you ask him, the Holy Spirit will show you wonderful things in the Word of God.

How can you find meaning in God's Word today?

Mentor

Follow my example,
as I follow the example of Christ.

1 Corinthians 11:1 ICB

Jackson sat in a circle of kids on the floor at church. It was Wednesday night, and they were in the middle of discussion time at youth group. They usually talked about the Scripture that was read, asked a few questions, and then spent some time praying for each other. Jackson really wanted to follow Jesus well and he was thankful for a place where he could learn how to do that. It was really helpful to be surrounded by people who wanted the same things he did.

God will put people in your life whom you can follow. Look for wisdom and guidance from others who also love Jesus. When you look to others and ask questions, you will realize you cannot do it on your own. This creates humility and teachability in your life. These are wonderful qualities to have because they will serve you well for your entire life.

Do you have people in your life to whom you can look for wisdom? If not, ask God to bring someone across your path who can help teach and guide you.

FEBRUARY

"Go and enjoy good food
and sweet drinks.
Send some to people
who have none.
Today is a hold day to the Lord.
Don't be sad.
The joy of the Lord
will make you strong."

NEHEMIAH 8:10 ICB

Honest

Kings are pleased when what you say is honest.
They value people who speak what is right.

PROVERBS 16:13 NIRV

Bryce walked in the door after being at a sleepover at his friend's house. He was tired from staying up all night and he was worried about seeing his mom. When she walked into the kitchen, he asked her if they could talk about something. They sat down at the table, and he explained that he had watched a movie with his friend he knew he wasn't allowed to watch. He knew he'd done the wrong thing, but he also knew that talking to his mom about it was better than hiding it.

It is always better to be honest. You will always be rewarded for your honesty. You might see that reward soon or it might come later, or even when Jesus comes back. No matter the timing, God always honors those who tell the truth. Truth brings freedom while hiding our mistakes only creates shame.

Is there something in your life
you should be honest about?

Incredible

The sky was made at the LORD's command.
By the breath from his mouth, he made all the stars.

PSALM 33:6 NCV

Jacob's family went camping every summer. One of his favorite things to do was sitting around the fire at night, eating s'mores, and watching the stars. Each time he was in awe over how bright the stars are—a million sparkling speckles he didn't normally get to see back home in the city. As they watched, Jacob's dad would strum a few chords on the guitar, and they might sing a worship song or two. Jacob loved that time with his family, praising God for his incredible creation.

Take some time to look around the world you live in. God's creation is wonderful, and it proves to us how good he is. When you thank him for what he has made, you will be reminded of his power and might.

What can you see around you reminds you
of how incredible God is?

Rejoice

Let the fields and everything in them show their joy.
Then all the trees of the forest will sing for joy.
They will sing before the Lord because he is coming.
He is coming to judge the world.
He will judge the world with fairness
and the nations with truth.

PSALM 96:12-13 ICB

Andrew was counting down the days until his birthday. He and his friends were going to have a campout in his backyard. They'd roast hot dogs, make s'mores, and hang out around the firepit. He couldn't wait. He was looking forward to the party with so much excitement it was hard to sleep. He'd wake up in the mornings and count how many days he still needed to wait. It was going to be the best birthday yet!

Birthdays, holidays, special occasions—there are so many different reasons to rejoice. We look forward to these events because we know they are good and we will enjoy them. If we can anticipate the goodness of a birthday, imagine the kind of celebration that will happen when Jesus comes back. The entire world and all of creation will be overjoyed. The Bible says that even the trees will sing for joy.

How can you celebrate the good things
Jesus has done even before he comes back?

Answers

Now we see but a faint reflection of riddles and mysteries as though reflected in a mirror, but one day we will see face-to-face. My understanding is incomplete now, but one day I will understand everything, just as everything about me has been fully understood.

1 Corinthians 13:12 TPT

Max sat in the kitchen with his mom. She was sitting in front of her computer, resting her head in her hands. She looked frustrated, so he asked her what was wrong. She said she was struggling through an issue at work and it was making her day stressful. Max was always surprised when his parents got stuck on something; he was still pretty convinced they could do anything. His mom sighed and explained that being an adult doesn't mean you know everything or everything is easy to understand.

In the same way, no matter how long you walk with Jesus, there will always be things you don't fully understand. God knows this and he has promised to give you full understanding when Jesus comes back. Then, everything will make sense. In the meantime, sometimes life can feel confusing or frustrating, but this doesn't mean God doesn't know what is going on.

Even when you don't understand what God is doing, how can you honor him with your actions?

Real

So stop telling lies. Let us tell our neighbors the truth,
for we are all parts of the same body.

EPHESIANS 4:25 NLT

Misha kicked a soccer ball across the room. It bounced off
of the wall and knocked over a picture frame, breaking it on
the floor. His mom was out for the afternoon, and he knew
when she got back, she would be upset. He cleaned it up and
tried to place it back where it was. When she got home and
saw it, she asked what had happened. Misha denied knowing
anything and so did his brothers. Frustrated that no one was
telling the truth, she took away the TV until someone owned
up to it. Misha knew his lie was affecting his brothers, but he
really didn't want to get into trouble.

It's important to tell the truth because it can impact those
around you. Your behavior isn't just about you. The way you
act can have a positive or negative impact on the people
around you. Lying creates an environment where trust cannot
thrive. Strive to be someone who tells the truth because you
love others. When you speak words that are real and true,
you care for others by building dependability and trust.

How can you practice honesty
even when it's uncomfortable?

Lively

Don't act thoughtlessly,
but understand what the Lord wants you to do.

EPHESIANS 5:17 NLT

Tyler stomped around his house. He was frustrated and annoyed. When his mom asked him what was wrong he replied that he was fine. It was obvious he wasn't fine. He continued to huff and puff and eventually his mom said to him, "Tyler, this is ridiculous. You know you aren't fine. Let's figure this out." Tyler knew his heart didn't feel right, but it was easier to ignore it than to try to fix what was wrong.

The Bible tells us to make sure we don't act thoughtlessly. This means we should be paying attention to what is going on around us and also to what is going on inside of each of us. It's important to be aware of what is in your own heart. Stay lively and ready for action anytime you notice something that does not honor God. Learn how to ask for forgiveness quickly and trust that God will always help you when you need it. Don't try to hide your sin or pretend that everything is fine. Let God help you with your mistakes and he will teach you how to follow him well.

Why is it bad to try to ignore sin?

Endure

The LORD is good. His faithful love continues forever.
It will last for all time to come.

PSALM 100:5 NIRV

Emmett had been told to clean out his room. He was slowing
going through each pile of items, sorting out what to keep
and what to get rid of. As he did, he remembered what
each thing had meant to him. There were forgotten toys
he'd barely touched in ages, books he'd enjoyed for weeks,
treasures he'd held dear for years, and certain mementoes
he'd had for longer than he could remember. He had loved
each item for a different amount of time and for different
reasons. Eventually, each time, his interests turned toward
something else.

The love of God has no end. He will never grow tired of you.
He will never stop loving you. This can be difficult to wrap
your mind around. As humans, we don't really understand
the concept of forever. Everything we know is limited. We
change our minds often and we don't understand endurance
the way God does. Nothing on Earth lasts forever. Without
understanding, all we can do is worship. His love is beyond
our understanding. Praise him for loving you so much you
can't even comprehend it.

How can you thank God today for his unending love?

Steady

Watch where you're going! Stick to the path of truth,
and the road will be safe and smooth before you.

PROVERBS 4:26 TPT

Nazar went hiking with his family. They'd been walking for
a while, and he was ready for some excitement. The trail had
been basically the same the entire time. After he turned a
corner he decided to see what things were like beyond the
well-worn path. He ventured into some trees and figured he'd
catch up with his family in a bit. After an hour of wandering
and a few panicked moments, he realized that maybe this
wasn't the best decision he'd ever made. He missed the
smooth and clear path the trail provided.

In the same way, God has created a path of truth for you to
walk. He knows exactly what your life will look like, and he
will be faithful to guide you if you let him. As long as you are
following Jesus you will always be on the right path, and he
will keep you steady. Learn how to listen for his voice and
to know the difference between what he says and what the
world says.

How can you practice hearing God's voice today?

Improve

So let us do all we can to live in peace.
And let us work hard to build up one another.

ROMANS 14:19 NIRV

James didn't always feel like being nice to his sister. She was quite a bit younger than him, and she often did things that really annoyed him. He was slowly learning how to be kind to her even when he didn't feel like it. At first the idea of responding to her with patience seemed completely impossible. Sometimes she just drove him crazy! But each time he chose to be patient and slow to anger, it got a little bit easier. He was proud of himself and the work he had done.

Peace takes work. Treating each other with kindness takes practice. People don't get along by accident. The more you pay attention to loving others well, the more you will improve. If you are struggling with one person in particular, try asking God to change your heart. He loves teaching his children how to love each other. Pray for the person who frustrates you and ask God to guide you in encouraging them.

How can you choose peace when it
would be easier to just be frustrated?

Focus

"The one who endures to the end will be saved."

MATTHEW 24:13 NLT

Benjamin ran across the finish line in gym class. He was the first person to finish their laps and it felt really good. He loved winning even when it wasn't a real competition. As he watched the rest of his classmates file in, he took notice of some of the slower runners. They didn't seem any less pleased with themselves than he was. In fact, some of them seemed even prouder of their accomplishment. He joined in with his class to cheer to them on.

Christianity is not a competition. It doesn't matter who crosses the finish line first, second, or third. All that matters is that you finish. Your race could be slow and full of obstacles. If you don't quit, you win. If you cross that finish line with your eyes on Jesus, you win. Instead of comparing yourself to others, keep your focus securely on Jesus.

Is there anything distracting you
from keeping your focus on Jesus?

Reward

We must not become tired of doing good.
We will receive our harvest of eternal life at the right time.
We must not give up!

GALATIANS 6:9 ICB

Cole was tired. He didn't feel like mowing the lawn anymore. After all, it was Saturday and he'd rather be at the lake. The sun beat down on him as he walked the final few passes across the yard. When he finished putting the lawnmower away, his dad met him outside with a smile and a tall glass of lemonade. It was cool and refreshing, just like jumping in the lake would be later. His dad knew how hard he'd worked, and he was happy to reward him.

In the same way, God sees you persevering. He knows that following him is hard sometimes. He knows sometimes you would rather be doing something else than what God asks of you. If you do not give up, he will reward you. He will graciously help you each step of the way. You can depend on him to lead you all of your days, and you can depend on him to be true to his promises.

When you are tired of following Jesus,
how can you build up your perseverance?

Stable

From long ago no one has ever heard of a God like you.
No one has ever seen a God besides you,
who helps the people who trust you.

ISAIAH 64:4 NCV

Clint knew he could rely on his dad. He was always there when he needed him. If Clint had a problem, the first thing he did was talk to his dad about it. Clint knew he could trust his dad because he had proven his trustworthiness. For his entire life, he had been faithful to show up. He wasn't perfect, but he never let him down when it counted.

It is good to have people in your life who you can trust. But no matter how great they are, they aren't perfect. God will never break your trust. He is trustworthy. This means he will do what he says; he is stable. You can trust in him because he is perfect. He has proven he loves us by sending Jesus to die on the cross. He made such a great sacrifice so we could be sure of his love for us.

Did you know you can always rely on God?

Significant

"Do not be afraid. I will set you free.
I will send for you by name.
You belong to me."

ISAIAH 43:1 NIRV

Liam sometimes felt lost in the mix. He had a big, loud, happy family. He loved them so much but sometimes he felt like no one noticed him. There were a lot of schedules to coordinate, and he knew his parents were doing their best. He just wished he could have a little more of their attention.

You are important to God. You are significant to him. It doesn't matter how many people there are on this earth; he sees you. He is a good Father who notices and cares for each of his children. He does not have limited resources like our earthly parents do. He does not have to divide his time or share responsibilities. His power has no limits, and his love has no bounds. You belong to the Creator of the entire universe.

If you truly understood your significance to God, what would change in your life?

Love

Most importantly, love each other deeply, because love will
cause people to forgive each other for many sins.

1 PETER 4:8 NCV

Jon sometimes had a temper. It was hard for him to make
good choices when he was angry. He was learning to do
better, but he still made mistakes. He was thankful for his
family who never gave up on him. They loved him every day,
even when he was angry. They encouraged him and were
kind when he apologized.

No one is perfect. We all make mistakes every day. When
you love someone well, you can keep loving them even when
they mess up. Jesus is the perfect example of this. He didn't
wait for us to be perfect to save us. He died for us while we
were still sinners. He continues to love you even when you
do the wrong thing over and over again. You can be like
in Jesus in the way you love others. Just because someone
makes a mistake doesn't mean you give up on them or stop
loving them.

Who in your life has shown you a love like Jesus?

Reliable

Teach those who are rich in this world not to be proud
and not to trust in their money, which is so unreliable.
Their trust should be in God, who richly gives us
all we need for our enjoyment.

1 TIMOTHY 6:17 NLT

Alan felt overwhelmed. For most of the morning he tried
find something to make himself feel better. No matter what
he tried, he couldn't seem to shake off his negative feelings.
Finally, he sat down with his dad and tried to explain how he
felt. His dad calmly asked him if he'd prayed about it. Alan
laughed and shook his head, "Well, that would be a good
idea, wouldn't it?" He knew he could rely on God, but he
often forgot to even ask for help.

You can rely on God. He is big enough to take care of all
you need. He is generous with everything he has. As his son,
you are an heir to the kingdom of God. Instead of trusting
in money or things that make you feel good, put your trust
in your Father. He is more reliable than anything else. He is
the Sovereign One. This means he controls everything. But
he is not in control like an angry ruler or a cruel dictator.
He is kind, generous, patient, and loving. You just need to
remember to rely on him.

Have you ever forgot to ask for help?
How can you practice trusting in God?

Serious

The time is near when all things will end. So think clearly
and control yourselves so you will be able to pray.

1 PETER 4:7 NCV

Sully was anxious for his grandparents to get to his house.
They lived really far away and Sully didn't get to see them
very often. They had been preparing all week for their
arrival. His mom had filled the fridge with their favorite
foods, and they'd rearranged their rooms to make sleeping
more comfortable for everyone. Sully had picked out his
favorite movies for movie nights and had picked a book to
read with his grandma.

Just like your family might prepare for a guest to visit, you
can prepare for Christ. The day is coming when Jesus will
return. He'll come back to earth and make all things right.
It's important to take that seriously. While you wait for him,
do your best to honor him with the way you live. You can
prepare for Jesus by praying and reading the Word. Listen to
the Holy Spirit and do your best to follow him.

If Jesus returned tomorrow,
how would you prepare today?

Civil

Let the words you speak always be full of grace.
Learn how to make your words what people want to hear.
Then you will know how to answer everyone.

COLOSSIANS 4:6 NIRV

Levi sat in math class on a Friday afternoon. Everyone was restless and ready to go home for the weekend. As the afternoon went on, he noticed other students getting more and more disruptive. They were joking around when they should have been working and were talking while the teacher was trying to go over the lesson. Normally Levi would have joined in with his classmates, but he noticed how his teacher looked stressed as well and he hoped that keeping his mouth shut might help.

What you say is important. It's also important to know when not to speak. Being polite and kind can change someone's day for the better. Your words are powerful. It can be tempting to try to sound cool or to puff yourself up with your words. Instead, let others be the ones who praise you, and not yourself. Let the things you say be encouraging and mindful.

How can you practice being polite
with your words today?

Brilliant

What he does is glorious and splendid.
His goodness continues forever.

PSALM 111:3 ICB

Carson walked home from school after a long day. As he took each step, he could feel his mind relaxing, and his focus went from his schoolwork to the world around him. He felt the sun on his face, and he was looking forward to spending the afternoon outside. He loved being outdoors. It was where he most understood God's love. If God could make the world so incredible and brilliant, then he must care about us very much.

If you pay attention, you will see God's brilliance everywhere. Everything he has made is good and glorious. The world is full of evidence of his love for you. Take a moment today to look around. Look at all he has done for us. In his great power he could have made the world however he wanted but he chose to make it beautiful for you to enjoy.

What are five things that show you
God's love and goodness?

Trustworthy

You will keep in perfect peace
all who trust in you,
all whose thoughts are fixed on you!

ISAIAH 26:3 NLT

Axel had a lot on his mind. He was worried about a presentation at school. His dog was sick. His best friend was moving away, and he was tired of struggling to get along with his sister. He was just worried about a lot in life. His mom would tell him to trust God and he tried but he wasn't sure how to do that.

God is trustworthy. He is true to his word. All throughout the Bible you can see where he kept his promises. If he did it once, he will do it again because he is consistent and he never changes. When you trust in him, you will have peace because you will be assured he is the one who is in control. You don't have to worry your way through life because he wants to carry your burdens. Trusting God can be as simple as talking to him about your worries and asking him for help.

What promise of God's can you cling to today?

Unafraid

Anyone who shows respect for the LORD has a strong tower.
It will be a safe place for their children.

PROVERBS 14:26 NIRV

Brad hated being in the dark. He knew it was a common fear, but he still felt silly about it. He was headed to camp in one week and he felt nervous about looking childish around his friends. His dad was helping him memorize some Scripture he could say to himself when he felt afraid. "Anyone who shows respect for the Lord has a strong tower." No matter how big or small his fears were, he knew God would surround him and keep him safe.

God pays attention to your fears. He doesn't tell you they're silly and he doesn't tell you to get over it. His Word says he will protect you and comfort you. As you follow him, you will learn he is always by your side and will never leave you. You can be unafraid because the Creator of the entire universe has your back.

When you are afraid, how can you find comfort in God?

Steadfast

They will not live in fear or dread of what may come,
for their hearts are firm, ever secure in their faith.

PSALM 112:7 TPT

Leo watched quietly out the window as his family drove up
the driveway of their new house. His dad's job had brought
them to a completely new state hundreds of miles away
from the home he grew up in. His parents had explained
what a good thing it was for their family, but he was really
struggling to care about that. He was worried, mad, afraid,
and just plain sad.

The Bible never promises if you follow Jesus your life will
be easy. But it does promise that your faith in him will
bring you comfort and security no matter what you face.
No matter what turns the path of your life will take, you
can remain steadfast in Jesus. That means even when your
circumstances change, you do not feel insecure or tossed
about. Even when you are upset, sad, afraid, or worried, you
can trust that God never changes, and he is by your side.

Is there something in the future you are worried about?
Ask God to replace your worry with steadfastness.

Enough

"You must not covet your neighbor's house. You must not
covet your neighbor's wife, male or female servant, ox or
donkey, or anything else that belongs to your neighbor."

EXODUS 20:17 NLT

Dylan was spending the afternoon at his friend's house.
The longer he was there the worse he felt even though their
house was full of incredible things. Dylan's friend had the
latest video games, a trampoline, a giant Lego collection, and
a TV in his room. Dylan went home feeling like he should
have all of those things as well. He felt something stir in his
stomach. It was a queasy feeling that made him think he
wouldn't be happy until he had more fun stuff.

Coveting means desiring something that doesn't belong to
you; it's a lot like jealousy. When you begin to covet what
other people have, you will quickly become unhappy with
whatever you do have. It doesn't matter if you have what you
need; you'll become convinced it just isn't enough. Living
this way will only lead you to unhappiness. A coveting heart
can never be satisfied. Instead, ask God to fill your heart with
thanksgiving for what you have already.

Have you been coveting certain things
in other people's lives? Seek to repent and
to replace jealousy with thankfulness.

Unique

You created the deepest parts of my being.
You put me together inside my mother's body.

PSALM 139:13 NIRV

Eli knew his parents loved him. He knew deep down
that was true, but he didn't always feel it. He was part of
a pretty big family, and it was easy to kind of get lost in
the mix. Everyone was busy, trying to manage their own
responsibilities. Sometimes Eli wondered what his place was.
He didn't always feel like he belonged.

You were deliberately created. No part of you is an accident.
No matter how you feel about yourself, you are God's
workmanship. You were uniquely created in the image of
God. He made you, on purpose, and with great love. Even
when the world seems chaotic, he sees you. He turns his eyes
toward you with care and attentiveness. There might be days
you feel looked over, but God is always aware of you.

Is there a part of your life that feels overlooked?
Can you practice talking about it
with God who sees you?

Charity

God supplies seed for the person who plants. He supplies bread for food. God will also supply and increase the amount of your seed. He will increase the results of your good works.

2 CORINTHIANS 9:10 NIRV

Seth hated doing group projects. He often felt like he did all of the work while the rest of the group just skated by. He was concerned enough about his own grades to make sure the slack got picked up. He didn't want the group to fail and so he often ended up doing more than his fair share of the work.

There are no unfair group projects in God's kingdom. He sees every single good work you do. He says he will give you what you need and will makes sure you are taken care of. There will always be rewards for following God's instructions. You might see those rewards here on Earth or you might see them when Jesus returns. Either way, God is faithful to his children. He has charity for you. This means he helps you because he wants to, and because it's ingrained in his very character to take care of you. He is not obligated or forced.

In what ways have you seen God take care of you?

Helpful

The Lord God said, "It is not good for the man to be alone.
I will make a helper who is just right for him."

GENESIS 2:18 NLT

Willem looked at his parents. He saw how they loved each
other, and it made him feel thankful and safe. Some of his
friends didn't have both parents living at home and he knew
how lucky he was. He watched how his parents treated each
other and he noticed how they took care of each other.

God made marriage and he designed it perfectly. A godly
marriage is one where both people honor and support each
other. This mutual respect glorifies God. When you selflessly
love someone else, you can teach them about how much God
loves them. Having a helper in life is a great gift. While you
are many years away from marriage, you can still thank God
for good examples of healthy marriages. You can also pray for
your future wife. Even though it seems very far away, you can
ask God to protect her and teach her how to live a godly life.

Who in your life has shown you what it looks like to
have a godly marriage? Thank God for them and ask
him to bless their relationship.

Eager

You should continue following the teachings you learned.
You know they are true, because you trust those who
taught you. Since you were a child you have known the
Holy Scriptures which are able to make you wise. And that
wisdom leads to salvation through faith in Christ Jesus.

2 TIMOTHY 3:14-15 NCV

Jett had been reading his Bible lately. If he were honest with
himself, he would say that he was confused and even a bit
frustrated. He grew up being taught about God but now
the more he read, the more he just had a lot of questions.
Some things didn't make sense to him, and some things even
seemed to contradict each other. A lot of what he read was so
different from what he saw in the world, and he didn't know
what he was supposed to do. He was afraid if he asked about
it people would think he wasn't a good enough Christian.

Eagerly search for truth! Read the Bible and ask questions. If
you find something you don't understand, dig deeper. If you
find something you don't like, discuss it with someone you
trust. God is not afraid of your questions. He is bigger than
any doubts or frustrations you might have. He wants to equip
you and encourage you. He is not annoyed when you don't
understand. In fact, questions show humility and create further
dependence on God. That is always a good thing.

How can you become good at asking questions?

Self-control

Better to be patient than powerful;
better to have self-control than to conquer a city.

PROVERBS 16:32 NLT

Cooper wanted to win. It didn't matter what the activity was; he wanted to be the best. He noticed though, sometimes his desire to win grew bigger than his desire to be kind or respectful. Sometimes when he lost, he would be so angry he didn't know what to do with himself. He was thankful for his dad, who would sit and pray with him and together they would talk about how to value doing the right thing over winning. It was hard for Cooper, but he was learning that winning is not the most important thing in the world.

God's kingdom does not match up with the world. A lot of things in God's kingdom are the opposite of what the world might tell you. Those who desire power and control will struggle with Christianity. Following Jesus is based on the realization that God is the one with ultimate power and control. As you walk with God you will see it is better to surrender to his greatness than to seek after your own.

Have you ever left goodness behind and instead let the desire to win take over? How can you develop self-control in that area?

Considerate

God's grace has been given to me. So here is what I say to
every one of you. Don't think of yourself more highly than
you should. Be reasonable when you think about yourself.
Keep in mind the faith God has given to each of you.

ROMANS 12:3 NIRV

Michael learned a lot from watching how his parents lived.
He had noticed lately how much time they spent taking care
of others. They were constantly doing things like dropping
off groceries for people in need or shoveling their neighbors'
driveways. When he asked them how they had time for that
they would reply, "God will give us what we need." They
didn't seem to be worried about whether or not they had the
time or money to help. They just did it. Michael knew he was
lucky to have parents who cared so much for others.

It can be really easy to become self-centered. This means you
only think about yourself. God has called us to a different
standard. He said it is more important to think about others.
It takes faith to be considerate of others because you have
to trust that God will take care of you. When you believe he
will provide for you, you can have the freedom to put others'
needs before your own.

What is one way today that you can take care of the
needs of someone else before your own?

MARCH

"Don't worry,
because I am with you.
Don't be afraid,
because I am your God.
I will make you strong
and will help you.
I will support you
with my right hand
that saves you."

ISAIAH 41:10 ICB

Polite

Tell them not to speak evil things against anyone. Remind them to live in peace. They must consider the needs of others. They must always be gentle toward everyone.

TITUS 3:2 NIRV

Karl sat at the dinner table with his family. They were all discussing some current events. As his brother was talking about the actions of a specific person, Karl interrupted with a loud, "I hate him!" He continued to talk negatively about how much he couldn't stand this particular person and why. When he stopped talking, he looked up and his dad was staring intently at him. He explained that what Karl said was wrong. "That man," his dad said, "is deserving of your respect and kindness, even if you disagree with him. Your words say more about you than they do about him."

Everything you say matters. Your words are powerful and can either create life or death. Be mindful of what you say. This means to take the time to choose your words carefully. Be polite to everyone. The actions of others shouldn't change the way you speak even if they can't hear you. Everyone, no matter what, is deserving of kind words. It isn't your job to decide what other people need or deserve. God said we are to be gentle with everyone.

Have you ever said something because someone, in your mind at least, deserved it?

Potential

Jesus has the power of God, by which he has given us everything we need to live and to serve God. We have these things because we know him. Jesus called us by his glory and goodness.

2 PETER 1:3 NCV

Bruce didn't feel very prepared. He had forgotten about a science test and hadn't studied all week. Science was his least favorite subject, and he knew that to do well on the test he needed to have gone over his notes a lot. He wasn't ready and he hated that feeling.

Feeling like you can't do something the right way can be really discouraging. Knowing you don't have what you need can make you feel small, insecure, or anxious. When it comes to serving God, he has given you a great gift. He has given you everything you need to follow Jesus. You are already prepared because of what God has done. When it comes to serving God and honoring him with your life, you don't ever need to feel like you aren't equipped. You've got the potential to do exactly what is needed because God, in his power, has set you up perfectly to do it.

Does knowing you are already prepared change how you feel about serving God?

Pure

These troubles come to prove that your faith is pure.
This purity of faith is worth more than gold,
which can be proved to be pure by fire but will ruin.
But the purity of your faith will bring you praise and glory
and honor when Jesus Christ is shown to you.

1 PETER 1:7 NCV

Walker's class was on a field trip to the local nature center.
They were learning about how maple syrup was made. He
had a solid interest in pancakes, so he watched intently as
they carried heavy buckets of sap over to the fire. As they
poured the sap into the pan, they first put it through a
filter. They explained that this made sure there weren't any
impurities in the sap. Little things can fall into the bucket
during collection, but you don't want them to be in your
finished product.

Difficult things in life can act just like that sap filter.
Sometimes when troubles come, they can help highlight
other issues so you can deal with them. On a hard day you
might realize you have been impatient or you use angry
words when you are upset. As you let God purify your faith,
you will be able to honor him even more. Just like filtering
impurities out of sap, your faith can be purified and can grow.

How can you change your perspective to look at
troubles as an opportunity to grow?

Responsive

Stay alert! Watch out for your great enemy, the devil.
He prowls around like a roaring lion,
looking for someone to devour.

1 PETER 5:8 NLT

Jared wanted to follow Jesus for the rest of his life. The
older he got the more he realized his relationship with Jesus
would require him to be diligent. He was learning how to
see God working in his life and he was also beginning to
see how Satan wanted to keep him from God. There were
opportunities each day to either choose what would honor
God or to do otherwise.

You are part of something real, wonderful, and incredible.
You get to have a relationship with the Creator of the
heavens and the earth. It's up to you to daily respond to what
God has done for you. Until Jesus comes back, you also need
to be aware of his enemy, the devil. Satan's greatest goal is to
separate you from God. Pay attention to anything that causes
you to turn away from Jesus.

Have you been diligent in your relationship with Jesus?
How can you choose to honor him each day?

Quiet

I am standing in absolute stillness,
silent before the one I love,
waiting as long as it takes for him to rescue me.
Only God is my Savior, and he will not fail me.

PSALM 62:5 TPT

Silas worried a lot. He worried about all of the things that could go wrong in a day and he worried about what the future might hold. He constantly had something on his mind that was making him anxious. Lately, he had been learning how to cast his cares upon Jesus. When a thought overwhelmed him, he had been practicing how to hand it over to God. He imagined taking his frustration, wrapping it up in a box, and literally putting it in God's hands. It seemed silly but it really helped Silas to let go of stress.

Does your mind ever feel like a storm? Have you ever felt anxious or overwhelmed? In those moments God can help you to be still. Turn toward him and let him quiet your heart. He will rescue you when you need it. He doesn't want you to be lost in your emotions. He is a kind Father and he wants to give you peace. You can give your worries to him, and he can quiet your heart.

Is there something making you anxious today
that you can hand over to God?

Heir

Since we are his true children, we qualify to share all his treasures, for indeed, we are heirs of God himself. And since we are joined to Christ, we also inherit all that he is and all that he has. We will experience being co-glorified with him provided that we accept his sufferings as our own.

ROMANS 8:17 TPT

Austin followed his dad into his workshop. Recently he had been teaching Austin how to use all of the different tools he used as a woodworker. Austin's dad built custom furniture and he was really skilled at his job. The workshop felt like a wonderland to Austin, full of things to do and explore. Because of his dad, he had access to all of it.

You are part of a family much larger than you might know. As a follower of Jesus, you have been adopted into God's family. As a child of God, you get to share all of his treasures and resources. Just like Austin had access to the tools his dad owns, you have access to all of the goodness God has to offer. You are an heir to the kingdom along with Jesus. Because of God, you have incredible privileges you wouldn't have otherwise!

How does knowing you get to share in all of God's treasures change the way you pray and communicate with God?

Humble

Always be humble and gentle. Be patient with each other,
making allowance for each other's faults because of your
love. Make every effort to keep yourselves united in the
Spirit, binding yourselves together with peace.

EPHESIANS 4:2-3 NCV

Wes got home from school one day and his little brother was
crying. When he asked what was wrong, he sadly replied, "I
took five dollars out of your room." He looked so ashamed.
"Mom caught me and said I had to tell you myself." Wes ruffled
his brother's hair and laughed. He explained he wasn't mad
and in fact, he'd done the same thing to their older brother
when he was younger. "Everyone makes mistakes," he said.

No one is perfect. We all make mistakes and God asks us to
be kind to each other, even when someone does the wrong
thing. He says to "make allowances for each other's faults."
This means we are to treat each other with understanding
and realize we will all mess up from time to time. Being
humble means realizing you make just as many mistakes as
the person next to you. When someone around you does
something wrong, remember how you want to be treated
when you make a mistake.

Are you aware when God is using you
to give grace to someone else?

Drift

Don't let me drift toward evil
or take part in acts of wickedness.
Don't let me share in the delicacies
of those who do wrong.

PSALM 141:4 NLT

Mark sat in the principal's office. He was listening to his parents and the principal talk to him about bullying. He'd been caught saying something horrible to a classmate and now he was dealing with the consequences. Mark was kind and a good friend. He even surprised himself by what he had said. But he had to admit that lately he'd been hanging out with kids he normally didn't. He'd been laughing at their rude jokes and sitting silently instead of standing up for the kids they hurled insults at. Now, Mark found himself acting the same way they did, and it had snuck up on him.

It's not often a person follows Jesus and then one day just decides not to live the right way. There isn't a sudden switch from good to wrong. Oftentimes it's the small decisions you make each day that lead you down the wrong path. This is why God reminds us to be on guard. He knows we are likely to desire things we shouldn't and so he graciously shows us how to honor him. Each good decision adds up to a lifetime of being faithful.

Is there any sin creeping up on you slowly?

Knowledge

I pray that your love will grow more and more. And let it be based on knowledge and understanding. Then you will be able to know what is best. Then you will be pure and without blame for the day that Christ returns.

PHILIPPIANS 1:9-10 NIRV

Charlie was working on a school project with Bill, a boy in his class. The partners had been assigned by their teacher. Charlie had never spent time Bill and didn't really know him at all. As they worked together, they realized they actually had a lot in common. If they hadn't spent all of that extra time together, Charlie never would have known how cool Bill was. He was thankful for a new friend.

Just like you need to spend time with other people to get to know them, you need to spend time with God. The more you get to know God, the more you will love him. This is what the Bible means when it says your love should be based on knowledge and understanding. You don't need to just love God because someone tells you to, or it seems like a good idea. Spend time with him and get to know him. He wants to have a relationship with you. As you understand more about who God is, your faith will be strengthened, and your knowledge will grow.

How can you spend time getting to know God today?

Inspiration

The Lord has filled Bezalel with the Spirit of God.
The Lord has given Bezalel the skill, ability and knowledge
to do all kinds of work. He is able to design pieces
to be made of gold, silver and bronze.

EXODUS 35:31-32 ICB

Connor wasn't really sure what he wanted to do when he was older. "What do you want to be when you grow up?" was a common question and he never really felt like he had an answer. Everyone around him seemed to have really specific ideas about who they would be, but Connor felt undecided.

Everybody has been given different gifts. Your particular gifts or talents might not be obvious to you right now. It's okay to grow into who you are. Not everyone has a clear idea of who they are, especially at your age. The Bible is full of people like Bezalel who honored God with the gifts he had given them. As you get older you'll learn what inspires you and how you most like to spend your time. Ask God to talk to you about how he created you. When you use the gifts he has given you, you honor him. It is a type of worship to enjoy and utilize the unique the talents or skills God has placed in of you.

How can you trust God with your future
and honor him with the gifts he has given you?

Needed

Some parts of the body that seem weakest and least important
are actually the most necessary. So, God has put the body
together such that extra honor and care are given to those
parts that have less dignity. This makes for harmony among
the members, so that all the members care for each other.

1 Corinthians 12:24-25 NLT

Devon and his mom were working on a puzzle. They did one
every Christmas and this year was no exception. The picture
this year was intricate, and it had been difficult to get a lot
of it done. Even though it was slow going, Devon loved the
satisfaction of finding the perfect fit each time. Each piece on
its own didn't look like much but all together, a really cool
picture was made.

You are an important part of the body of Christ. Who you
are specifically is needed for the purpose of God. Each
part of the body works together to honor God. The body
of Christ is like a puzzle, each piece fitting perfectly where
it belongs. It doesn't work to swap the pieces around and
expect them to fit somewhere differently. God is most
glorified when we each fulfill our own role and respect the
roles of others. There isn't one puzzle piece that is more
important an another; each one is needed and important.

Do you know what your role is in the body of Christ?
If not, how can you learn what it is?

Worthless

Not only those things, but I think that all things are worth nothing compared with the greatness of knowing Christ Jesus my Lord. Because of him, I have lost all those things, and now I know they are worthless trash. This allows me to have Christ.

PHILIPPIANS 3:8 NCV

Gavin felt frustrated. His friends at school were all talking about what they had received for their birthdays that year. Gavin's family didn't really give a lot of presents, at least not over the top ones like his friends were talking about. When he asked his dad why, he replied that, "There are more important things in life." He didn't like that answer but he knew his dad was right.

The greatest treasure you could find on earth is nothing compared to a precious relationship with Jesus. All of the goodness the world has to offer is still not as good as he is. It is all worthless when compared to knowing Jesus. Be careful not to get caught up in desires for more and more stuff. Instead, ask God to show you the goodness that is found in Jesus. As you get to know him more, you will see how much more valuable your relationship with him is than anything else in your life.

Do you ever feel like you don't have enough?
How can you replace that feeling with
the satisfaction of knowing Jesus?

Permanent

Lord, remind me how brief my time on earth will be.
Remind me that my days are numbered—
how fleeting my life is.

Psalm 39:4 NLT

Joel was twelve years old. He hadn't even started high school yet and he felt like he had all the time in the world to live the life he wanted. That's why he felt frustrated with his parents when they told him to use his time wisely. Why should he think at all about that kind of thing? He was just a kid and all he had as time, stretching out in front of him.

No matter how long your life is, you have a permanent home with Jesus. Because you believe in your heart Jesus is the son of God and he was raised from the dead, you will spend eternity with him. You will live forever. Your time on earth is very temporary but your home in heaven is permanent. It will never end. Some days or seasons might seem long but overall, life is very short. Ask God to teach you how to spend your time wisely.

Does knowing your time on earth is limited
change the way you want to spend your time?

Mercy

Have mercy on me, O God,
because of your unfailing love.
Because of your great compassion,
blot out the stain of my sins.

PSALM 51:1 NLT

Riley sat in his room. He was grounded for the night for calling his sister some unkind names. He knew he had done the wrong thing but at least he was better off than his older brother. He was grounded for a whole month. He had snuck out the house and lied to his parents. "At least I'm not that bad," Riley thought. Comparing himself to his brother made him feel better.

You don't deserve the forgiveness of God. You don't deserve his compassion or his unfailing love—nobody does. That is what makes God so incredibly merciful. He gives us goodness we do not deserve. Understanding God's mercy should cause you to worship him and be thankful. It should also cause you to have humility because you are just as undeserving as the person next to you no matter how good you think you might be. God's mercy allows you to see everyone around you equally because we all fall short of God's standards. You are not a better or worse sinner than the person next to you. All have sinned and fall short of the glory of God.

How can you let God's mercy create humility in your life?

Attentive

These Jews were better than the Jews in Thessalonica.
They were eager to hear the things Paul and Silas said.
These Jews in Berea studied the Scriptures every day
to find out if these things were true.

ACTS 17:11 ICB

Pascal had been arguing with his sister a lot. One day his mom sat him down and they had a long conversation about it. When it came down to it, Pascal thought since she was younger than him she should listen to what he had to say. His mom explained that treating her that way because of her age was unfair to both of them. She said he would miss out on truly knowing his sister if he constantly needed to be in charge because she was younger.

Make it your goal to be attentive to those around you. Each person you encounter can teach you something different about who God is. We are all made in his image and therefore we each reflect different aspects of his heart. If you pay attention you will begin to see God in everyone you meet. Age, talent, wealth, and intelligence don't matter. Every single one of God's people is made in his likeness and has something beautiful to offer.

How can you honor each person you meet
no matter how different they are from you?

Beauty

He has made everything beautiful in its time. He has also given people a sense of who he is. But they can't completely understand what God has done from beginning to end.

ECCLESIASTES 3:11 NIRV

Kyle was a problem solver. He loved a challenge. He liked to come across a problem and then work to find the best possible answer. He felt accomplished when he could cross something off of his list and he knew he had done his best. When his Sunday school teacher said he would spend his whole life getting to know God he felt baffled. How could he spend that much time on one thing?

You could read the whole Bible word for word, and you still wouldn't fully understand God. Until you meet him face-to-face, there will always be parts of him that are beyond you. He is intricate, incredible, and beautiful, and we cannot fully know him. This is not supposed to be overwhelming. It means you can never run out of things to explore. God is not a problem to solve. He wants a relationship with you. Everything he does is beautiful, and you have the privilege of spending your life walking with him and learning about him.

Have you been looking at Christianity as something to figure out or as a relationship with your Creator?

Celebrate

Celebrate with praises the God and Father of our Lord Jesus Christ, who has shown us his extravagant mercy. For his fountain of mercy has given us a new life—we are reborn to experience a living, energetic hope through the resurrection of Jesus Christ from the dead.

1 PETER 1:3 TPT

Dean was bored at church. He felt like he'd been learning the same things his entire life. He'd heard the same stories over and over. His teacher, on the other hand, seemed constantly excited about what God was doing. He figured that must be an adult thing but at the same time, he couldn't let go of the idea that maybe she understood something he didn't.

God has done amazing things and we should celebrate them. It's exciting so see how wonderful he is and how he has given us such great hope. If you ever feel like Christianity is boring, celebrate God. Take some time to really thank him for the greatness of all he's done. As you praise his good works, you can't help but be excited about who he is.

Can you think of three reasons from this past week to celebrate God?

Logic

"The minds of these people have become stubborn.
They do not hear with their ears, and they have closed
their eyes. Otherwise they might really understand
what they see with their eyes and hear with their ears.
They might really understand in their minds
and come back to me and be healed."

MATTHEW 13:15 NCV

Most of Clay's friends didn't believe in God. They said there wasn't any proof that God existed. But Clay argued that the proof was everywhere. He saw how God made the world and all of the people in it. He saw how intricately creation worked together and he knew that couldn't have been an accident. The best explanation was someone had made it with great thought and care.

God is at work all around you. All of creation points to him. Everywhere you look there is evidence of who God is. It is logical to see that creation must have had a creator. If you pay attention you will always see God working. As you see what he is doing, praise him for who he is. Thank him for his good works and know that your faith makes him proud.

How can you honor God for all he has done?

Same

God is not a man, so he does not lie. He is not human, so he
does not change his mind. Has he ever spoken and failed to
act? Has he ever promised and not carried it through?

NUMBERS 23:19 NLT

Galen knew the Bible said God loved him. When he read the
Word, he believed that it was true, but sometimes he had a
hard time applying it to his own life. Sometimes he felt like
maybe he was forgotten. He knew great believers like Noah,
or David, or Paul had special relationships with God, but he
didn't see how that could also be true for him.

You can trust the Word of God. He keeps his promises, and
he always tells the truth. He doesn't change his mind. He is
always the same. If he says he loves you, then that is true for
eternity. If he says he cares for you, then he always will. He
is the same God to you as he was to the people who lived
in biblical times. You can depend on who he is. No matter
how you feel on any given day, God is always the same. Your
feelings and opinion cannot change who he is.

When you feel far from God, how can you
rely on his Word instead of your feelings?

Diligent

The LORD says, "I will save the one who loves me. I will keep
him safe, because he trusts in me. He will call out to me, and
I will answer him. I will be with him in times of trouble.
I will save him and honor him. I will give him a long
and full life. I will save him."

PSALM 91:14-16 NIRV

Wally's mom made him feel loved and secure. She was
always there when he needed her, and she always had an
encouraging word to say. He knew he could ask her for help
no matter what, and she would do her best to protect him. If
his mom who was just human could love him so greatly, how
much more must God love and cherish him?

God is diligent in the way he loves you. He will never
quit loving you. When you call out to him, he will always
respond. At some point, the people around you will
disappoint you no matter how much they love you. But God
will never leave you hanging or forget what you asked for. He
is faithful and true, and he will always be attentive to you.

How can you love others diligently in order to
display the diligent love of God?

Delight

Enjoy serving the LORD,
and he will give you what you want.
PSALM 37:4 NCV

Trev adored his little brother. There was a pretty big age
gap between them, and he took his role as the older brother
pretty seriously. He looked out for him, helped his mom
keep an eye on him, and delighted in making him laugh.
Each day after school he would scoop him up and give him
a silly little gift, a doodle on a paper, a pinecone, or a trinket
he'd found. They were pretty meaningless things, but they
put the biggest smile on his cute little face.

If it delights you to give a gift to someone you love, can you
imagine how God feels about giving good gifts to you? He is
the perfect giver, and he loves to bless his children. He is not
a genie who will grant your wishes. He is a kind Father who
is generous with all he has. As you walk with God you begin
to see all the ways, big and small, he has blessed you.

Can you think of five ways God
has been generous toward you?

Renewed

Do not be shaped by this world. Instead be changed within by a new way of thinking. Then you will be able to decide what God wants for you. And you will be able to know what is good and pleasing to God and what is perfect.

ROMANS 12:2 ICB

Grant hadn't been a Christian very long. He decided last summer he wanted to follow Jesus, but he still feels new at it. Sometimes he still acts like he did before. He knows that some of his actions are wrong but it's really hard to change. He is really trying to do the right thing but sometimes he just feels stuck.

As a follower of Jesus, there will be times in your life when you are tempted to live in a way that doesn't honor God. Sometimes this will be super clear and other times you might feel unsure of what the right thing is. The more you walk with God, the more you will learn to think the way he thinks. As you spend time with him, he will renew your thinking. With practice and an understanding of the Word, it will become easier to know what is right and what is wrong.

Think of an area of your life that has been shaped by the world. How can you begin to honor God in that area?

Daring

Some trust in chariots. Some trust in horses.
But we trust in the LORD our God.

PSALM 20:7 NIRV

Luis had big plans for his life. He loved to think about all of the things the future could hold. Sometimes when he shared his ideas, he knew that people thought they were a little bit over the top. Luis didn't care. His parents often reassured him that he'd been given hopes and dreams by God. "If God placed a dream in your heart," they'd say, "then he'll help you to do it."

Dare to trust in God. Something you need might seem impossible but that doesn't mean God can't manage it. He is the God who created the world, can raise the dead, and can cause the blind to see. He can do miraculous things. You'll never know if you don't ask. Take all of your wild and impossible dreams and put them in God's hands.

Do you need a miracle in a certain area of your life? Put it in God's hands and trust that he can handle it.

Recognized

Don't let anyone think less of you because you are young.
Be an example to all believers in what you say, in the way
you live, in your love, your faith, and your purity.

1 TIMOTHY 4:12 NLT

Marshall quietly walked to the front of the classroom. His
youth pastor had asked him to share his testimony on
Wednesday night and the time had arrived. He knew God had
done a lot of great things in his life this past few months, but
he still felt so nervous to talk about it. Most of the room was
filled with high school kids and next to them, Marshall felt so
small. Surely, they must know more about God than he did.

Your age might limit you from doing certain things like
driving or having a job, but it can't limit you in your
relationship with God. It doesn't matter how old you are, you
can honor the Lord with everything you say and do. You don't
have to be a grown up to be an example to other believers.
Your faith, even now, can inspire and encourage people who
are three, four, or five times your age. God recognizes what is
in your heart, not how many years you've lived.

Have you been timid because of your age?
How can you honor God and let your faith be
recognized no matter how old you are?

Brightness

The Son is the shining brightness of God's glory. He is the exact likeness of God's being. He uses his powerful word to hold all things together. He provided the way for people to be made pure from sin. Then he sat down at the right hand of the King, the Majesty in heaven. So he became higher than the angels. The name he received is more excellent than theirs.

HEBREWS 1:3-4 NIRV

Hayden loved a good story. He felt like the first book he read opened up a whole different world to him. He could get lost in a book and barely stop to eat a snack. He loved how the characters would be woven together and how the hero would always come through in the end. With each book he tore through he longed to be a part of a great adventure.

God has created an incredible story that you get to be a part of. You are in the middle of an intricate reality, woven together by the Creator of the universe. From when Adam breathed his first breath until the return of Jesus, God has been at work. He appointed his Son to redeem all of mankind. It isn't a fairy tale or a fantasy novel. Jesus is the best hero you will ever read about.

How can you look for the brightness of Jesus in the story you are living right now?

Glory

Through our faith, Christ has brought us into that blessing of
God's grace that we now enjoy. And we are happy because of
the hope we have of sharing God's glory.

ROMANS 5:2 ICB

Travis adored his grandfather. They were very close, and
when he passed away Travis was devastated. He was angry,
sad, hurt, and frustrated. He really had no idea how to cope
with such a big loss. His mom would pray with him and
thank God that one day he would wipe all of their tears away
and they would all be together again, sharing in the glory of
God. She said their faith was strong enough to carry them
through any hardship, even one as horrible as this.

God said Jesus would come back again and make all things
right, and we believe he will. Reminding yourself of his
promises can give you strength when life is hard. Looking
forward to seeing God's glory can help you persevere when
you encounter difficult things.

When has the hope of God's glory carried you
through something difficult or painful?

Deliverance

His light broke through the darkness and
he led us out in freedom from death's dark shadow
and snapped every one of our chains.

PSALM 107:14 TPT

Milo lost the book he was reading. He was just about to go
to bed, and he wanted to read it. He wandered around the
house looking for it but couldn't see it anywhere. It was dark
and he kept stubbing his toes and getting frustrated. His
search would have gone a lot better if he just would have
turned on a light.

Living your life without Jesus is like searching for something
in the dark. Jesus is light. It doesn't make sense to wander
around in the dark when you don't have to. You have been
delivered from darkness. As a follower of Jesus, you get to
walk in the light. You don't have to wander through life
unable to see clearly and being confused about what to do.
Jesus' light brought you salvation and he wants to guide you
all of your days.

How does Christ's deliverance change how you live?

Awesome

Let us be thankful, because we have a kingdom that cannot be shaken. We should worship God in a way that pleases him with respect and fear.

HEBREWS 12:28 NCV

Cormac felt like everything around him was changing. His older brother was leaving for college, his family was moving to a new house, and his best friend would be away for the summer for the first time. Cormac felt nervous, like there was nothing he could rely on. He felt unsteady and worried about what the next few months would look like.

You serve an awesome God. As a follower of Jesus, you are part of a kingdom that cannot be shaken. You stand on a firm foundation that will never crumble. Anytime you feel unsteady you can lean on Jesus. No matter how much changes in your life, God does not change. He is your anchor in the storm. He is worthy of your time and your worship. Today if you feel unsure, turn your eyes to Jesus and realize he is big enough to hold you up.

When your world feels shaky, how can you depend on God instead of worrying about the future?

Authentic

My goal while I was with you was to talk about only one
thing. And that was Jesus Christ and his death on the cross.
When I came to you, I was weak and very afraid
and trembling all over.

1 CORINTHIANS 2:2-3 NIRV

Shane felt like he should tell his friends about Jesus. His
relationship with God was so important to him and was a
huge part of his life. He realized one day he wasn't sure if his
friends even knew he was a Christian. He wanted to talk to
them about who God was, but he felt nervous. What if he did
the wrong thing or explained something in the wrong way?

Even someone like Paul, one of the greatest apostles of the
New Testament, was afraid to share about Jesus sometimes.
He knew he wasn't any more skilled than the next person. His
skill isn't what gave him confidence. It was the power of Jesus
that gave him confidence to share the gospel everywhere he
went. The Bible is full of authentic people who don't lie about
their weaknesses. They are very aware of their weaknesses
and praise God for the strength he gives them.

Have you been relying on your skills
or on the strength of God?

Capable

"You have a large number of skilled stonemasons and carpenters and craftsmen of every kind. You have expert goldsmiths and silversmiths and workers of bronze and iron. Now begin the work, and may the LORD be with you!"

1 CHRONICLES 22:15-16 NLT

Philip was supposed to build a bird house for Boy Scouts. He tried to get the right sized boards, but he wasn't supposed to use the saw without his dad's help. He tried to attach the roof pieces together, but he couldn't find the right screws. It seemed like every part of the project was out of his reach. He felt frustrated and annoyed. How was he supposed to get it done if he didn't have any of the right supplies, tools, or help?

God told the people in 1 Chronicles to build the temple. He was the one who gave them the job. Notice he didn't give them instructions and then just leave them alone to figure it out. He also made sure they had the tools and the skilled workers that were needed. He will do the same thing for you. He doesn't ask you to follow his instructions and then just leave you alone. If he has told you to do something, he will also make sure you are capable of doing it well. He will equip you to follow what he has asked.

Is there an instruction from God that seems too big for you? How can you trust that he will give you what you need to do it?

Extra

Every gift God freely gives us is good and perfect,
streaming down from the Father of lights,
who shines from the heavens with no hidden shadow
or darkness and is never subject to change.

JAMES 1:17 TPT

Isaac knew he had a lot to be thankful for. He had everything he needed. He was safe, warm, and cared for. When he prayed at nighttime, those were the things he thanked God for. So, when his dad asked him to list ten things he was thankful for, he felt baffled. He'd only ever thought about the few obvious things in his life. As he started to pay attention, little things started popping up everywhere. He thanked God for the way his little brother laughed at a joke, or how his mom sang when she cooked. He thanked God for how his friend taught him a new soccer trick and that his dog was always happy to see him at the end of the day.

Every good thing in your life is from God. He knows exactly what you need, and he is the one who provides you with it. He brings beauty and joy to your life that goes beyond what you need to survive. He is a not just good at taking care of you, he is also generous and kind.

What are two gifts God has given you
that you've never thanked him for?

APRIL

The LORD gives me strength
and protects me.
He has saved me.
He is my God,
I will praise him.
He is my father's God,
and I will honor him.

EXODUS 15:2 NIRV

Aware

Keep me from looking at worthless things.
Let me live by your word.

PSALM 119:37 NCV

Maverick was spending the afternoon at his best friend's
house. When they turned on the TV to watch a movie he
cautiously asked which one they were going to watch. His
friend said a title Maverick knew his parents wouldn't be okay
with. "Could we pick something else?" He asked confidently.
He didn't really like asking that question, but it was better
than explaining to his parents that he broke their trust.

It is good to be aware of what you are looking at. What kind
of books are you reading? What kind of movies or shows are
you watching? Does what you're looking at honor God and
create goodness in your life? Or is it making you anxious,
unkind, or angry? The things you allow into your mind
directly impact your life. It might seem frustrating to have
rules or limits but it's what is best even for adults. Maturity
isn't being able to do what you want. It's being capable of
making good choices when no one is making you do it.
Make good choices and it will pay off.

Are you looking at anything that isn't creating goodness
in your life? How can you make better choices?

Follow

Then Jesus said to his disciples, "If any of you wants to be my follower, you must give up your own way, take up your cross, and follow me."

MATTHEW 16:24 NLT

Amos was on a hiking trip with his family. They were exploring a national park they had never been to before. As they walked along the trail, Amos couldn't help but think it would be more fun to just wander around exploring than it was to follow the map they'd been given. He was about to tell his dad that when they approached the edge of the hill they were climbing. The sun crested the cliff, and the view took Amos's breath away. It was incredible. He was glad they had made it to the top in time to see that amazing moment.

Being a Christian is just like following someone on a hike you've never been on. If you insist on your own way, you will likely get lost and miss out on the view at the end. In order to have a faith that perseveres, you've got to admit that Jesus' way is better than your own way. You can't follow him well if you still think you can live without him. Admitting your need for salvation through Christ is the first step to following him for the rest of your life.

Are you following Jesus or are you trying to make your own path?

Adoption

You have not received a spirit that makes you fearful slaves.
Instead, you received God's Spirit when he
adopted you as his own children.

ROMANS 8:15 NLT

Joey loved spending time at his best friend's house. He really
felt like part of their family. One evening after eating dinner
with them he carried his plate to the kitchen sink. His friend
looked at him and said, "Guests don't have to do the dishes,
Joey." His dad called from the other room, "You're not a
guest; you're family. Wash your plate." Joey smiled. Washing
the plate didn't bother him at all. He loved being treated like
he belonged.

You have been adopted into the family of God. He has called
you his son and you get to have the Creator of the universe
as your Father. You are not a slave, a guest, or just a follower.
You are a cherished and beloved child. When you talk to God,
you can approach him just like you would approach your own
dad. You can be confident he loves you and values you. You
are wanted and you have a place in the family of God.

Have you viewed your relationship with God
as a father and son or as a slave and a master?

Abundant

They eat well because there is more than enough in your house. You let them drink from your river that flows with good things.

PSALM 36:8 NIRV

Drew was ready for lunch, so he decided to make himself a sandwich. He went to the fridge, grabbed a slice of cheese, and slapped it between two pieces of bread. As he took a bite, he watched his brother make his sandwich as well. He started by spreading some mustard on a slice of bread, then he added a slice of cheese on each side. Next, he layered on several kinds of deli meat and a juicy slice of tomato. He ripped off a crunchy piece of lettuce and put it in the middle. He finished it off with some avocado slices and even added a piece of bacon that was left over from breakfast. As Drew finished his sandwich, he couldn't help but wonder why he had settled for just cheese when there were all of those delicious options.

God has unlimited resources. He is a God of abundance. This means he has more than what is needed. He is not the kind of God who just does something part way. He has provided us with more blessings than are necessary. He doesn't just want you to survive, he wants you to thrive and flourish in the life he has given you. You can expect big things from God.

Have you been expecting "just enough" from God when he wants to bless you with abundance?

Pleasing

"I hope I continue to please you, sir," she replied.
"You have comforted me by speaking so kindly to me,
even though I am not one of your workers."

RUTH 2:13 NLT

Kevin wanted to please God, but he really didn't know where to start. He decided to follow Jesus after going to a church camp and while he was excited about it, he didn't know how to do it. He didn't have any Christians in his family, and he had learned about God from his friend who had brought him to camp. He knew in his heart that following Jesus was good and right, but he felt alone and unsure of how to do the right thing.

Do your best to live a life that pleases God. If you are unsure of what that looks like, start with the Bible. Read through the pages to find examples of how people honored God. You'll see how people treated others, how they worshiped, and how they lived out their everyday lives. Read Genesis to learn about the beginning of the earth and how God called his people. Read through Psalms to learn how to worship. Read through Proverbs for wisdom and advice. Read the Gospels—Matthew, Mark, Luke, and John—to learn about Jesus' life. The Word is a wonderful gift and will always point you back to how loved you are and how great God is.

Have you ever felt like you
don't know how to follow Jesus?

Completion

God began doing a good work in you.
And he will continue it until it is finished
when Jesus Christ comes again.
I am sure of that.

PHILIPPIANS 1:6 ICB

Andy was working on an art project for school. He was trying to paint a portrait of his family and he just couldn't get it right. He kept messing up the same thing. Each time he did it wrong he would angrily crumple up his paper and start over. After enough frustration, he decided to paint something different.

God isn't finished with you. Even if you live to be a hundred and ten years old, there will never be a point when God says he is done with you. This should give you hope because it means he will never give up on you. He will always be willing to teach you and help you. Even if you make the same mistake over and over like with Andy's painting, God doesn't give up on you. He will continue to have grace and mercy for you until you are complete, which for each of us is when Jesus comes back again.

Is there an area of your life
you thought God had given up on?

Right

> "I, Nebuchadnezzar, give praise and honor and glory to the King of heaven. Everything he does is right and fair, and he is able to make proud people humble."
>
> DANIEL 4:37 NCV

Jonah argued with his sister. "I'm right!" she yelled. "No, I'm right!" he countered back. They each knew the other person wouldn't let it go, and so back and forth they went.

Eventually Jonah got frustrated enough that he stomped off to his room, angry and bothered. He couldn't even remember what they were fighting about.

You serve a God who is always right. Not only is he right in action but he is also right in attitude and character. He is not prideful or arrogant. Have you ever met someone who seems to think they are never wrong? Usually with people, that kind of attitude comes with rudeness, but it doesn't with God. He is never wrong, but he is always gracious, always merciful, and always kind. The fact that he is always right, and he is always loving means you can put all of your trust in him because he will never fail.

> Do you trust that God is never wrong,
> or have you doubted his goodness?

Effective

The prayer of a godly person is powerful.

JAMES 5:16 NIRV

Tanner sat at the dinner table with his family. His dad was talking about some current events. Whenever Tanner thought about politics, he thought about how nice it would be to just call up the president and ask him about it. Wouldn't it be great to be able to talk directly to the one with the most power in the situation?

You don't have a direct line to the president, but you do get to communicate with the Creator of the entire universe. You get a direct audience with the most powerful King there has ever been. He is never too busy for you or too far away for you to reach. Your prayers are effective. This means they work. God hears you and he responds. This doesn't make him like a genie who gives you whatever you want. It means he is an attentive Father who is always available. When you pray it is like you are saying to God that you believe who he is and he is powerful enough to help you.

Have you viewed prayer as effective or as boring?

Acceptable

Abraham was, humanly speaking, the founder of our Jewish
nation. What did he discover about being made right with
God? If his good deeds had made him acceptable to God, he
would have had something to boast about. But that was not
God's way. For the Scriptures tell us, "Abraham believed God,
and God counted him as righteous because of his faith."

ROMANS 4:1-3 NIV

Peter had been reading his Bible lately. He was learning
about all of the heroes of the faith. As he read, he felt a bit
intimidated. It seemed like these people all did incredible
things. They performed miracles and watched God do big and
mighty acts. Peter wondered if he would ever be able to live a
life like that. He didn't feel good enough or important enough.

We don't read about Abraham because of all the great things
he did. He didn't have special talents or incredible skills that
made him different from anybody else. He is considered a
biblical hero simply because of his great faith. Everything he
did was because he believed God would keep his promises.
Your talent and success aren't what pleases God. Your faith
in who he is and that he will do what he says is what makes
you acceptable to God.

Have you been leaning on your own talents
or on the greatness of God?

Convinced

I am absolutely sure that not even death or life can separate
us from God's love. Not even angels or demons, the present
or the future, or any powers can separate us. Not even the
highest places or the lowest, or anything else in all creation
can separate us. Nothing at all can ever separate us from God's
love. That's because of what Christ Jesus our Lord has done.

ROMANS 8:38-39 NIRV

Adam loved working with his dad. Most weekends they
spent their spare time working on cars in the garage. No
matter what kind of project they were working on, Adam
enjoyed the tasks that were involved. His dad was a good
teacher. He was kind, patient, and genuinely loved having his
son help him. Adam knew no matter what, even if he made a
mistake, his dad would kindly teach him how to fix it.

If an imperfect person like a parent can make you feel so
loved, then can you imagine the greatness of God's love for
you? There is absolutely nothing that can separate you from
the love of God. When you are convinced of this truth, it
changes the way you live. When you are sure you are never
alone you will have confidence to do the things God asks of
you. When you are convinced that his love never leaves you, it
becomes a joy to live a life that honors him.

Is your obedience to God done out of love
or because you think you have to?

Rational

Stay away from anger and revenge.
Keep envy far from you, for it only leads you into lies.

PSALM 37:8 TPT

Blake was so angry with his brother. He had told their parents about the time when Blake had broken his mom's favorite picture frame and then lied about it. In his anger he decided to get back at his brother. Blake told himself it was the fair thing to do and went ahead and swiped his brother's baseball glove, hiding it under his own bed. Blake thought that watching his brother search for the glove would make him feel better, but it only made him feel worse. Revenge was not all it was cracked up to be.

When you feel angry, it is tempting to let that anger control what you do. It feels like the most important thing to let it take over your decisions. You might want to yell at people and make sure your opinion is heard, or you might want to bottle it up and store all of that rage in your heart. Neither of these options is good for you. Both will lead to bitterness and disappointment. When you feel angry the Holy Spirit can help you to be rational. He can point you to the wisdom and gentleness of God who is always slow to anger.

When you feel angry, what can you do to depend on the Holy Spirit instead of lashing out?

Rich

You are rich in everything—in faith, in speaking, in knowledge,
in truly wanting to help, and in the love you learned from us.
In the same way, be strong also in the grace of giving.

2 CORINTHIANS 8:7 NCV

Stewart knew his family always had what they needed. He
was thankful but also confused. His parents often talked
about how rich they were, and he didn't understand. In his
mind, if they were so rich then how come he constantly
had a list of things he wanted but he couldn't get? If they
were rich, then shouldn't he have more video games, and
shouldn't they take better vacations?

Throughout your life you might have twenty, two hundred or
two hundred thousand dollars in the bank. No matter what
the dollar amount is, you are a rich man. This is because you
have been given an inheritance from God. As his son, you
are an heir to the entire kingdom. It might sound cheesy, but
the richness you have in Christ is better than an overflowing
bank account. No amount of money can buy what you have
been given through your salvation in Jesus.

How does being rich in Christ change
the way you think about money?

Important

"If you tenderly care for this little child on my behalf,
you are tenderly caring for me. And if you care for me,
you are honoring my Father who sent me.
For the one who is least important in your eyes
is actually the most important one of all."

LUKE 9:48 TPT

Evan often noticed when other people were sad. Especially
at school, he seemed to have a radar for when someone was
feeling left out or ignored. One of his favorite things to do
was to make people smile when they felt like that. He didn't
care what anyone thought of him, he liked to befriend people
whom everyone else seemed to think weren't good enough.
Just because there was something different about them didn't
mean they should be lonely.

It is normal to look at others and notice what is different
about them. We are all uniquely made by God. What's
important about our differences is that they have nothing
to do with value. Each person is equally valuable to God no
matter what the world might say. God says every person he
has made is equally important and worthy of a high level
of respect. When you respect other people despite their
differences, you honor God.

What can you do when you see someone
being devalued or disrespected?

Servant

"The greatest among you must be a servant."
MATTHEW 23:11 NLT

Gabe really wanted to sit in the front seat for his family's annual road trip. Each year they drove out to visit his grandparents a few states away. Sitting in the front meant he got to control the radio and help his mom decide where to stop for lunch. He also got to spend time with just the two of them, talking about anything and everything. As they loaded into the car, he noticed his sister walking toward the front. He knew she got car sick and the front was probably the best spot for her. That day, instead of fighting with her, he quietly climbed into the back. Today, he decided to let her have a turn without an argument.

When you choose to serve others, you are loving them in the same way Christ has loved you. He was the very best example of servant leadership. He is the Son of the most high God, yet he willingly came and laid his life down for a world full of sinners. His status is higher than yours will ever be, but he still took a lowly position and served everyone around him. If you want to follow Jesus, you will need to learn how to serve others with humility and selflessness. This means you will need to learn how to put the needs of others before your own.

How can you practice being a selfless servant today?

Saved

The message of the cross seems foolish to those who are lost
and dying. But it is God's power to us who are being saved.

1 Corinthians 1:18 nirv

Richard loved springtime. It was full of new life. Everything
was fresh and exciting. He loved watching the world around
him wake up after a long, cold winter. This time of year, his
mom would pick blooms from their yard and place them on
the kitchen table. The vase was a daily reminder that winter
didn't last forever. All of the new life around him made
him think about the new life he had in Jesus. His salvation
reminded him each day that God loved him.

You have been saved by what Jesus did on the cross. You
were once lost, but now you are found. Without Jesus, you
wouldn't be able to part of God's family. Your sin was in the
way but now you are free from sin because Jesus died in your
place. He took the punishment we all deserve. He paid the
price for our sins so we wouldn't have to.

How can you thank God today for your salvation?

Satisfied

Jesus said to them, "I am the Bread of Life.
Come every day to me and you will never be hungry.
Believe in me and you will never be thirsty."

JOHN 6:35 TPT

Benji's older brother was graduating high school this year.
He noticed a lot of people would ask him what he was going
to do after graduation. This made Benji think about his own
life. It felt like it would be forever before he'd be done with
school, but the thought still stressed him out. What would
he do? What kind of person would he be? What kind of life
would he live? There seemed to be so many options and he
really had no idea what he even wanted.

People are always looking for meaning. We were created to
long for more than what we see every day. As you get older
you see people spend all of their time looking for more
money, more success, and more happiness. The truth is no
matter how long you search, you will never be satisfied with
anything the world has to offer. True satisfaction only comes
from Christ. In him, you will find all you need. You could
live a thousand lives a thousand different ways but you will
never find what you want unless Christ is in the center of it.

When life's choices seem to overwhelm you,
how can you focus on being satisfied in Christ first?

Redemption

Through Christ, God has brought all things back to himself again—things on earth and things in heaven. God made peace through the blood of Christ's death on the cross. At one time you were separated from God. You were his enemies in your minds, and the evil things you did were against God. But now God has made you his friends again.

COLOSSIANS 1:20-21 NCV

Nate really wanted a new bike. Whenever he went to the store with his mom he would stare longingly at the rows of shiny, new bicycles. He had been saving his money, but he knew the price of the bike he wanted was still far more than he was able to pay. You can imagine his surprise when one day after school, he got home to see the exact bike he wanted parked in the front yard.

Comparing Jesus to a bicycle might seem silly but the basic idea is the same. You have been redeemed. You were separated from God by your sin but Jesus paid the price for you to be returned to him. Jesus made a way for you to be with God again. Because of him, you get to be where you belong. Jesus paid a price you could never have afforded. Your salvation is a gift from God. The price was completely out of your reach and God paid it anyway because of his great love for you.

Have you thanked God lately
for the price he paid for your sins?

Choices

My brothers and sisters, you were chosen to be free.
But don't use your freedom as an excuse to live under
the power of sin. Instead, serve one another in love.

GALATIANS 5:13 NIRV

Nicholas was home alone for the very first time. His mom
had a new job and it was the first day of summer. His parents
had decided he was old enough to stay home while she
worked. The whole day belonged to him, and he could do
whatever he wanted. The idea of freedom was so exciting.
He thought about raiding the pantry for cookies or maybe
watching a movie he normally wasn't allowed to watch.
Before he did, he caught himself. If he wanted to keep
staying home alone, he'd have to show his parents he could
make the right choices.

When you are very young, a lot of your choices are made
for you. Someone decides what you eat, where you go, who
you see, and how your time is spent. As you get older, those
decisions become yours to make. It shows maturity when
you can make the right choices without someone telling you
what to do. The same is true about your relationship with
God. It shows maturity when you can use your freedom to
make the right choices without being told what to do.

How do you choose to use the freedom
Christ has given you?

Trust

When I am afraid,
I will trust you.
I praise God for his word.
I trust God. So I am not afraid.
What can human beings do to me?

PSALM 56:3-4 ICB

Every year Colin looked forward to camping with his family. He loved sleeping in the tent, he loved swimming every day at the lake, and he loved exploring new trails when they would go hiking. The only thing he did not love was the dark. At some point, without fail, he would need to make his way to the bathroom in the dark. When he did, his dad would walk with him. As long as he was there, Colin was not afraid. He knew his dad could handle any surprises they might encounter in the dark woods.

You might trust your dad in a scary situation because you know who he is and what he can handle. The same is true about God. When you know who he is, how powerful he is, and how much he loves you, the only response is to trust in him. You can have confidence that he will keep you safe because he says he will, and he is true to his Word.

Is there an area of your life that would
be different if you trusted God with it?

Unshakable

Stand strong. Do not let anything move you.
Always give yourselves fully to the work of the Lord,
because you know that your work in the Lord is never wasted.

1 CORINTHIANS 15:58 NCV

Archie and his dad were building a tree house in their
backyard. They walked around the yard together, trying to
decide which tree was the best option. Archie picked one
near the back of the yard. His dad took one look at it and
said no. He explained it just wasn't big enough. Even if they
built the perfect house, the tree wouldn't be able to hold the
weight of it. They would need to pick a tree that was older,
stronger, and steadier.

You can stand firm because God is a steady foundation.
You are not strong because of your own skills or talents.
You are strong because of who God is. It's the same idea as
a well-built tree house on a tree that's too small. The quality
of the house doesn't matter if the foundation isn't strong.
Being unshakeable means no matter what life throws at you,
you stay grounded. Life doesn't have to be a rollercoaster of
emotions or an unpredictable storm. When you trust in Jesus,
he can keep you steady no matter what the circumstances are.

Have you been depending on your own strength
or on the strength of God?

Good

Taste and see that the LORD is good.
Blessed is the person who goes to him for safety.

PSALM 34:8 NIRV

Roberto took a deep breath and closed his eyes. The salty sea air filled his nose as warm water swirled around his toes. He felt happy, and he felt free. Once a year his family would visit the ocean, and he looked forward to it every time. He felt lucky to be able to experience something so wonderful. As he swam in the warm water, he thanked God for making a place that made him so happy.

God is good. There are an unlimited number of ways you can experience his goodness. You can feel the sun on your face on a beautiful day. You can watch a prayer be answered in the way you hoped. You can feel the love of a friend or family member. You can experience God's peace when you would normally be worried. God's goodness is not something you just think about. It is something you can actually taste, see, and feel in your heart and in the world around you. If you pay attention, you will see his goodness everywhere.

What is your favorite memory of God's goodness?

Unashamed

Make every effort to give yourself to God as the kind of person he will approve. Be a worker who is not ashamed and who uses the true teaching in the right way.

2 TIMOTHY 2:15 NCV

Navarro stood in line at a concert. It was really exciting because his uncle was a musician performing in the concert. He traveled around the country doing shows and this was the first one Navarro was able to attend. He didn't even need to have a ticket for the event. When he got to the door, he simply said who he was, and they let him into the event. He got in for free because of who he knew.

Jesus' death on the cross is what makes us presentable to God. It's just like getting into a concert for free because you know the lead singer. Without Jesus, we would never be good enough to stand before God. Jesus' sacrifice is why we can go to God without shame. We don't have to worry about whether or not we are good enough because Jesus' blood covers all of our mistakes. We are good enough because of what he did.

Did you know you have God's approval because of Jesus?

Teachable

> "I tell you the truth, unless you turn from your sins
> and become like little children, you will never
> get into the Kingdom of Heaven."
>
> MATTHEW 18:3 NLT

Craig love to learn new things. He loved to explore and read about things he had never heard of before. His mom sometimes called him a sponge and said she hoped he was always so teachable. When he asked her what she meant by that, she explained that she hoped he always had an attitude that was willing to learn instead of an attitude that insisted he was already the best.

You might feel like you have your entire life in front of you and a million things to learn. The truth is even as an adult, being teachable is one of the greatest attributes you can have. Just because you get older, doesn't meant the leaning stops. Being teachable means you don't think you already know everything. It means you are always willing to learn and grow. Being teachable protects you from pride and allows you to admit when you need help. This is especially important in your walk with God. Being teachable means you are constantly running to God for help instead of assuming you have life figured out.

How can you practice being teachable?

Prayerful

Always be joyful. Pray continually, and give thanks whatever happens. That is what God wants for you in Christ Jesus.

1 THESSALONIANS 5:16-18 NCV

Reggie's family prays before each meal. He also ends each day with a quick prayer, thanking God for various things. When his youth leader started talking about prayer being a conversation, he felt confused. To him, it was just something he did because he was told it was important. The idea that he could talk to God anytime and God would speak to him as well was new and kind of exciting.

You don't need to feel intimidated by prayer. It isn't something that makes you a better Christian because you cross it off of a to-do list. Prayer is like a conversation between you and your best friend, your father, or your teacher. Talking with God doesn't need to be planned or perfectly executed. It's the most natural thing in the world. Prayer is you talking with one who made you. He knows you inside and out and his love for you is never ending. You can tell him anything. He wants to hear from you.

How does your view on prayer change when you view it as a conversation and not a requirement?

Harmony

Make allowance for each other's faults,
and forgive anyone who offends you.
Remember, the Lord forgave you,
so you must forgive others.

COLOSSIANS 3:13 NLT

Owen and his older sister didn't get along. They fought and bickered and rarely spent time together that didn't include some kind of argument. He felt like she was always picking on him. She felt like he tried to annoy her on purpose. Around and around they would go, constantly frustrated and annoyed with each other. Lately his mom had been talking to them about forgiveness and harmony.

Making allowances for each other's faults means treating someone with kindness when they make a mistake because you know you make mistakes as well. It means having grace for others when they fail because of the grace God has given you. When you treat others in this way, you create harmony. Sometimes it is hardest to forgive the people who are closest to you. Forgiveness for the little things is just as important as the big things. Loving your sister with grace is just as pleasing to God as forgiving an enemy.

Have you been applying God's Word
to your simple, everyday life?

Promises

The Lord is not slow in doing what he promised—the way some people understand slowness. But God is being patient with you. He does not want anyone to be lost. He wants everyone to change his heart and life.

2 PETER 3:9 ICB

Arlo often heard people talking about how great everything would be when Jesus came back. His parents would talk about it at home, especially if they were going through something difficult. His pastor would preach about it on Sunday mornings. His youth leader would encourage them by saying things like, "One day, he will make all things right." Arlo had great hope for all God would do, but when he really thought about it, he felt frustrated. If God was big enough to fix everything, what was he waiting for?

If Jesus coming back means everything will be perfect, then you might wonder why he hasn't done it already. What is he waiting for? Has he forgotten about his promise? Not at all! God is patient and his timing is perfect. He wants everyone to know him. He will not give up and he will not get tired of waiting. He knows exactly what he is doing. He will come back at the perfect time when all of his promises have been kept. His patience is merciful.

Have you ever wished God would hurry up and solve the world's problems?

Holy

God has chosen you and made you his holy people. He loves you. So you should always clothe yourselves with mercy, kindness, humility, gentleness, and patience.

COLOSSIANS 3:12 NCV

Gabriel didn't feel like being kind to his sister. She was annoying him, and he had run out of patience. No matter how hard he tried, he just couldn't seem to muster up the ability to be loving toward her. Everything he said came out as frustrated. He knew this was wrong, and so he talked to his mom about it. She sat down with him and prayed. She asked that God would transform his heart and fill him with love for his sister.

You have been made holy because of what Jesus has done for you on the cross. You are holy because he is holy. You don't have to rely on your own talents or skills. It is not your job to make yourself perfect. The only perfection you need is the perfection of Jesus. He is the one who helps you to be merciful and kind. When you feel like you don't want to act in this way, ask for help. God loves to help his children. He is capable of changing your heart if you ask.

Have you been asking God for help, or have you been trying to solve your own problems?

Bound

Over all these good things put on love.
Love holds them all together perfectly as if they were one.

COLOSSIANS 3:14 NIRV

Jay sat on his grandma's couch. He was visiting her for the week and his time at her house was always extra special because she lived so far away. Today it was raining and so he was watching a movie, wrapped up in one of her quilts. He noticed all of the little squares were different pieces of fabric, all bound together into one big piece. The thread connected each piece and made it into something better than pile of little squares.

Love is what holds all of us together in Christ. We are all part of the family of God because of love. We are bound together just like the pieces of a quilt by the love of God. It connects us. When we have nothing in common, we have God's love. It is the one thing we can all agree on and focus on. Even though we are all different, God's love is steady and equal for everyone.

How does God's love make us all equal?

Honor

Be devoted to tenderly loving your fellow believers as
members of one family. Try to outdo yourselves in respect
and honor of one another.

ROMANS 12:10 TPT

Boden and his brother always had a competition going.
They were constantly trying to one up each other. To them,
beating the other person was their highest goal. It didn't
matter if it was a race to see who finished their homework
first, or who scored the most goals, or who called first dibs
on the front seat, they were always trying to outdo each
other. Their mom would chuckle and ask them to compete
over doing the dishes, buying birthday gifts, or figuring out
who could take the trash out the most times.

Can you imagine a world where we all try to outdo each
other in the ways we respect and honor others? What if,
instead of seeking success, acclaim, and wealth, each person
put the majority of their energy and resources into honoring
the people around them. The world would be a very different
place than it is today. This is the kind of world God had
in mind when he created man. His desire for us is that we
would love each other well and all of our actions would show
just how much we care for each other.

How can you outdo yourself in the way
you honor others today?

Represent

Whatever you do or say, do it as a representative of the Lord Jesus, giving thanks through him to God the Father.

COLOSSIANS 3:17 NLT

Grayson had been in Boy Scouts for years. This summer his group was joining troops from all over the state for a camping trip. As they prepared for the trip his leader explained to them that their actions represented their entire troop. He said he expected them to be kind, helpful, and brave. He said that when they acted in that way, it showed their troop had good attitudes and took the Scout values to heart. The actions of each person represent the group as a whole.

When you are part of a group or a team, your actions and words reflect upon everyone. In the same way, your actions and words in everyday life should represent who Jesus is. When you speak, your words should honor God. The way you treat others should show how Jesus would treat others. You have an opportunity to show the world the truth about who God is by living your life in a way that honors him.

Today, how can you represent Jesus well?

MAY

"Here is what I am commanding you to do. Be strong and brave. Do not be afraid. Do not lose hope. I am the LORD your God. I will be with you everywhere you go."

JOSHUA 1:9 NIRV

Friendly

Accept each other just as Christ has accepted you
so that God will be given glory.

ROMANS 15:7 NLT

Nathanial liked everyone he met. He was easy to get along
with and he genuinely enjoyed meeting new people. He was
friendly and welcoming to anyone who came across his path.
His dad said this part of Nathanial's personality was a gift
from God and it showed other people a little bit about who
God is. Nathanial was proud of that part of his personality
and tried his best to continue encouraging others.

We are supposed to treat each other in the same way Jesus
treats us. He is kind, loving, and accepting towards everyone.
He is friendly and welcoming. When you treat other people
in this way you glorify God. It is pleasing to God when his
children accept each other. Remember each person you
meet is made in his image and is important to God. There is
something inside of everyone that reflects who God is. If you
focus on those things instead of the things you don't like,
you'll begin to see everyone as a valuable creation, just like
God does.

How can you be accepting of others even if you don't
get along or they are different from you?

Adore

How right they are to adore you.

SONG OF SOLOMON 1:4 NLT

Parker knew that God was good. He'd been told all of his life that he was worthy of praise. The older he got the more he wanted to experience that for himself. He didn't want to love God just because his parents told him to. He began to spend a little bit of time each day asking God to teach him about who he was. As time passed, he found there was no shortage of reasons to praise him.

Everything about God is worth praising. There is no darkness in him. There is nothing about him that is bad or upsetting. He is fully good and fully worthy of being glorified. You could spend your entire life trying to experience his goodness and you wouldn't have enough time. As you walk with him you might have seasons of doubt or confusion. On those days, focus on what you know is true—God is good all of the time. Though life has its ups and downs, your adoration of God can carry you through any storm.

What is something about God you
haven't praised him for before?

Appreciate

I praise you because you remember me in everything, and
you follow closely the teachings just as I gave them to you.

1 CORINTHIANS 11:2 NCV

Julian woke up and wandered into the living room. His dad
was sitting there reading the Bible. When Julian sat next to
him, his dad began telling him about what he was reading.
He listened carefully and then asked a few questions. His dad
patiently answered him before they prayed together. Julian
was thankful for his dad. He knew he was lucky to have
someone who cared so much about his faith.

It is good to appreciate the people in your life who are
teaching you how to follow Jesus. They are investing in who
you are and are taking the time to help you mature. Life
would be much harder if you had to do it all on your own.
Today, take a moment to say thank you to someone who is
helping you in your relationship with God.

Who in your life is teaching you about Jesus?
How can you thank them today?

Bold

The thing I want and hope for is that I will not fail Christ in
anything. I hope that I will have the courage now, as always,
to show the greatness of Christ in my life here on earth.
I want to do that if I die or if I live.

PHILIPPIANS 1:20 ICB

Brand was walking home from school with a group of
friends. As they walked, they came to a point where
they could choose to stay on the sidewalk or cut across a
neighbor's property. If they took the shortcut they would be
home faster. Brand knew they weren't supposed to, though,
and this neighbor had asked their parents that they stop
cutting across their property. As his friends began climbing
over the fence, Brand bravely kept walking. He knew it was
important to do the right thing even when others weren't.

Following Jesus requires you to be bold. There will be times
when the decisions you make don't make sense to those
around you. As a Christian, you will have chances to honor
God in big ways and in small ways. Honoring God doesn't
always match up with what other people think you should
do. Sometimes you will have to be brave and stand up for
what you know is right.

When others do something you know is wrong,
how can you choose to honor God?

Community

"Where two or three gather together as my followers,
I am there among them."

MATTHEW 18:20 NLT

Anthony was having an especially rough week. His family was going through a really hard time. On Wednesday night he reluctantly walked into youth group. He really didn't feel like going but his mom thought it would be good for him. As he crossed the room his friends were immediately at his side. They saw by the look on his face that he wasn't doing well. As a group, they prayed for him and encouraged him. Anthony left feeling loved and cared for.

God designed each of us to need each other. Especially as you grow in your faith, you need other Christians to encourage you. You need a community around you who can help you live a life that honors God and support you when things are difficult. God says when his people gather together he is with them. He is a God who keeps his promises so you can be confident he will show up when you are with other believers. If you ask him, God will be faithful to give you a good community.

Do you have a community of Christians
to support and encourage you?

Shine

Then you will be pure and without blame. You will be children of God without fault among sinful and evil people. Then you will shine among them like stars in the sky.

PHILIPPIANS 2:15 NIRV

Brogan opened up his lunch at school. He saw his sandwich and was about to say something about it when he heard a wave of complaint rise up from the kids around him. Each person had something negative to say about what they were eating. He realized that when he chose to not complain he felt better, and he stood out for having a positive attitude.

Complaining and arguing isn't good for you. It creates frustration in your heart, and it makes you feel heavy. That is not what God wants for you. He wants your heart to be light and at ease because you trust in him. Complaining shows you are more worried about how you feel than about what would honor God. When you are filled with joy instead of complaint, you will shine.

How can you trust God for joy instead of being full of complaint today?

Refreshing

The generous will prosper;
those who refresh others will themselves be refreshed.

PROVERBS 11:25 NLT

Brock tried his best to always do the right thing. He really
tried to make good choices, but he often felt like no one
noticed. Sometimes he got tired of doing the right thing.
He wanted to be noticed and praised for the good things he
did. When he did something like helping his little brother
when his mom wasn't home, he wanted to be rewarded.
It sometimes felt like there wasn't a point to being nice to
others if they couldn't do anything for him.

God sees all you do. This isn't meant to make you feel like you
are being watched by a dictator or a boss. Instead, it should
encourage you that nothing you do goes unnoticed. Every
good thing, no matter how small, is noticed by him. When you
encourage others, God will encourage you. When you care for
others, God will care for you. Nothing is ever wasted in the
kingdom of God. You don't have to worry about keeping track
of your own good deeds, because God keeps the score, and he
is perfect at it. He will reward you for the good you do. When
you put the needs of others before your own, God in all of his
great power will make sure you are taken care of.

Does knowing that God sees what you do
encourage you to act with kindness?

Able

I can do everything through Christ,
who gives me strength.

PHILIPPIANS 4:13 NLT

Robert had never tried public speaking before. It wasn't
something he felt naturally good at, and he didn't really like
being the center of attention. When his teacher announced
they would need to write and deliver a speech for their end-
of-the-year project, he felt really nervous. He did his best to
prepare but when the day came, his mom could tell how unsure
he felt. She prayed with him before he left for school and
reminded him God would give him strength if he asked for it.

God is the one who gives you strength. He is the one who
created you and specifically gave you your talents and
abilities. Every little thing you are able to do is because God
has granted you the ability to do it. You can praise him for the
air in your lungs and the way your legs help you move. You
can praise him for your ability to sing or your ability to read a
novel quickly. He has designed every part of you. You are able
to get through each day because of what he is doing for you.
You are also able to tackle whatever comes your way because
of the strength he gives you. When you rely on him for his
strength, you will find you can do more than you realized.

Are you depending on God's strength
or your own to tackle new problems?

Rest

"I myself will go with you.
And I will give you victory."

EXODUS 33:14 ICB

Ezra sat in the car with his dad. He was on his way to a
birthday party. It was at a house he had never been to before
and was worried they would be late or they wouldn't be able
to find it. When he told his dad what he was worried about,
his dad replied with a smile, "Good thing I've got it all under
control." Ezra knew if his dad said it was okay, he could trust
his word.

You don't always need to know which way to go. Following
Jesus is actually more about trusting him than it is about
knowing a lot. He says he will always be with you and so you
can rest and know you are safe. When you feel anxious about
something, even if it is small, remember he is on your side
and promises you victory.

When you are worried do you rest in Jesus
or try to fix it on your own?

Glad

We laughed and laughed and overflowed with gladness.
We were left shouting for joy and singing your praise.

PSALM 126:2 TPT

Jonathan felt like he just couldn't measure up. No matter
how hard he tried, he felt like he was always doing the
wrong thing. He wanted to live a life that honored God but
he was tired of feeling like he was always messing up. One
day his mom sat him down and asked him if he knew God
was proud of him. She said to him, "God looks at you and
is full of joy! He is glad he made you and he wants you to
experience the joy he has."

God is not like a harsh ruler or an angry parent. He is not
looking down at you, watching to see if you do the right
thing. He is completely perfect. He is wise, powerful, and
yet also joyful. Have you ever thought about him being a
happy God? When you are full of gladness, that reflects who
God is, and he delights in it. You might have thought about
Christianity as full of rules or concepts that are hard to
understand. The truth is, it is also full of gladness. God is a
delight, and he wants you to experience that part of him.

Have you been viewing God as a harsh ruler
or a happy Father?

Consistent

"I will also bless the foreigners
who commit themselves to the LORD,
who serve him and love his name."

ISAIAH 56:6 NLT

Kim had decided to be a Christian when he was younger. He had attended church all of his life and he was looking forward to being baptized that summer at camp. When his dad asked him why he wanted to be baptized he responded, "Well, that's what Christians do right?" His dad explained to him that while it was good to publicly declare your faith, what mattered more was how you chose to declare your faith each day.

Being a Christian is more about consistency than it is about grand acts of faith. You will need to decide each day if you want to honor God. It is the small, everyday decisions that add up to a lifetime of following Jesus. Turn your attention to the goodness of God each day and in return for your consistency, you will grow in love for him.

Is your Christianity focused on big events
or faithful acts of service?

Decent

"Love your enemies! Do good to them. Lend to them
without expecting to be repaid. Then your reward from
heaven will be very great, and you will truly be acting as
children of the Most High, for he is kind to those who are
unthankful and wicked."

LUKE 6:35 NLT

Sami was busy putting his laundry away. It was Saturday
morning, and he was anxious to get his chores done so he
could play video games. Just as he hung up his last shirt,
he noticed a pile of his brother's clothes on the floor. He
thought about helping him out but then he remembered
how they had fought last night, and he decided if his brother
wasn't going to be kind, then he wouldn't be either. He didn't
think his brother deserved his help.

It is not always easy to be decent to people, especially to
those you might consider an enemy. You might change the
way you treat someone because you don't think they've
treated you the right way. The Bible says we are supposed to
love everyone. This means you should be kind to everyone
you meet, no matter how you feel about them. God is kind to
everyone, even those who are unthankful and wicked. When
you love other people equally, you are showing the world
who God is and how he operates.

Does the way you treat others depend on their actions?

Energy

Christ is the one we preach about. With all the wisdom we have, we warn and teach everyone. When we bring them to God, we want them to be like Christ. We want them to be grown up as people who belong to Christ. That's what I'm working for. I work hard with all the strength of Christ. His strength works powerfully in me.

COLOSSIANS 1:28-29 NIRV

Ben wanted to tell his friends about Jesus, but he wasn't sure how. He didn't want to say the wrong thing and he wasn't sure how they would react. He asked his dad for help and he told him something that really made a difference. He explained that words were great, but teaching people about Jesus is about more than words. Your actions say just as much about God as what you say.

Teaching other people about Jesus is an activity that is worthy of your energy. One of the best ways you can love others is to show them how much Jesus loves them. Sometimes this means talking to them directly about who Jesus is and sometimes it means showing them with your actions. You can be generous with your time, patient with people who are frustrated, and kind to people who are lonely. These are all ways that teach the world about who Jesus is.

How can you teach someone about Jesus without words?

Determined

When people are tempted and still continue strong,
they should be happy. After they have proved their faith,
God will reward them with life forever.
God promised this to all those who love him.

JAMES 1:12 NCV

Cash was tired of studying. His end-of-the-year science test was coming up and he hated science. He felt like there were too many terms and too many complicated processes. He had struggled through the class all year and he was nervous about failing the test. His mom knew he was worried and so she had been helping him study for the last two weeks. Even though he was sick of it, he worked harder than he had for any other class. He was determined to do a good job and on the day of the test, he knew his preparation had paid off.

Like most things that are worth working for, following Jesus takes determination. Determination means having an attitude that says, "I will not quit no matter what." Throughout your life, there will be many opportunities to quit on God. You might be tempted by what the world has to offer. You might be discouraged in your faith. You might get distracted by the pursuit of something you think is more important than Jesus. No matter what obstacles come your way, following Jesus will always be the best choice you can make.

Are you determined to live a life that honors God?

Equipped

I do live in the world. But I don't fight my battles the way
the people of the world do. The weapons I fight with are not
the weapons the world uses. In fact, it is just the opposite.
My weapons have the power of God to destroy
the camps of the enemy.

2 CORINTHIANS 10:3-4 NIRV

Henry was in the middle of a really difficult time. He had just
lost his grandfather and he didn't have any idea how to deal
with how sad he was. His grief felt like a heavy weight that
was too big for him to carry. One day as he cried, his mom
comforted him. She said to him, "This storm is really big,
but you have what you need to get through it. You have your
family to encourage you and you have the Word of God to
remind you of his goodness." Even though he had never been
this sad, his mom's word made him feel like he would be okay.

God has given you all you need to live in the world. He has
equipped you to stay faithful to him and to fight whatever
battles come your way. Because of the power you have in
Jesus, you can survive storms, you can fight temptation, and
you can weather discouragement. No matter what happens,
he is on your side, and he will fight with you. Be encouraged;
you are well equipped.

When you face hardship,
what weapons can you depend on?

Fearless

"Don't worry, because I am with you.
Don't be afraid, because I am your God.
I will make you strong and will help you.
I will support you with my right hand that saves you."

ISAIAH 41:10 ICB

"I can't do it," thought Leif. He was about to go away to sleepover camp for the first time and his mind of was full of doubt. His thoughts were clouded with all of the things that could go wrong and he felt overcome by nervousness. What if he didn't make any friends? What if he missed home too much? What if something awesome happened at home and he missed it? He had all sorts of concerns. The day before he left his dad sat down to pray with him. He reminded him that no matter what, God would be with him. He helped him to pray through each of his fears and Leif began to feel his anxiety melt away.

God doesn't ask you to be fearless because of how strong you are. He asks you to be fearless because of how strong he is. He wants to take care of all of your fears. Give them him, even if you have to do it a million times. You don't have to be afraid because God is on your side. You don't have to sit and wonder if you have what it takes or if you are capable. The creator of the entire universe has your back. Depend on him and he will make you strong. Trust in who he is, and he will support you.

Is there an area of life where you could be fearless?

Gift

It was only through this wonderful grace that we believed in him. Nothing we did could ever earn this salvation, for it was the gracious gift from God that brought us to Christ!

EPHESIANS 2:8 TPT

Steven sat with his dad at the park. They were eating ice cream together. As he enjoyed his triple scoop, he thought about how he didn't really deserve the treat. He'd gotten into an awful fight with his sister and spent most of the day frustrated and annoyed. When he told his dad he was sorry for what he'd done his dad looked at him and said, "You might not think you deserve a treat Steven, but I wanted you to have it, because I love you." Steven knew his dad's kindness was a gift that didn't depend on how he acted.

Your sin is too big for you to be able to pay for it yourself. Without Jesus' death on the cross, you would spend eternity without God. Jesus is the one who made a way for you to be saved. He did this for free and out of love. Salvation is a gift. It doesn't require you to pay anything. No matter how long you are a Christian or how much you mature in your faith, you should always be in awe about what Jesus has done for you.

Have you thanked God for the gift of salvation lately?

Hope

We are pressed on every side by troubles, but we are not
crushed. We are perplexed, but not driven to despair.
We are hunted down, but never abandoned by God.
We get knocked down, but we are not destroyed.

2 CORINTHIANS 4:8-9 NLT

Matt was tired. He was in the middle of the worst week of his
life. He was so discouraged by everything happening around
him he didn't think he'd make it to Friday. It was one of those
weeks when everything seemed to be going wrong. As he got
ready for school his mom could see how discouraged he was.
She prayed for him before he left, that he would know God was
with him, and that he would be encouraged by his presence.
Matt felt overwhelmed but he believed God would help him.

No matter what trial you might face, you will not be
overcome. You can have hope that God will always be with
you, fighting your battles, and keeping you safe. There is no
problem too big for him. There is no mistake he cannot deal
with. He is a God of redemption. This means he loves to fix
what is broken and make it whole again. Even on days when
everything seems to be going wrong, you can trust God is by
your side and will always be there for you to lean on.

Do you have a problem in life
you thought was too big for God?

Identity

He saved us because of his mercy. It was not because of good deeds we did to be right with him. He saved us through the washing that made us new people through the Holy Spirit.

TITUS 3:5 NCV

Troy was working on a school project. The topic of the project was "Who Are You?" Each student was supposed to put together a short presentation about how they would describe themselves. Troy had never really thought about it, and he was having a hard time coming up with ideas.

Your identity is who you are. Some people might say their identity is that they are a teacher, a mother, a basketball player, or a firefighter. No matter what types of things you do in life, your truest identity is that you are a child of God. You have received his great mercy and are part of his family. There will be many other ways to describe yourself but the most important one is that you belong to Jesus. If you are confident in that truth, then the other details of your life will fall into place.

How does having confidence in your identity in Christ change the way you live?

Kindness

Be kind and affectionate toward one another.
Has God graciously forgiven you?
Then graciously forgive one another
in the depths of Christ's love.

EPHESIANS 4:32 TPT

Montana was really frustrated with his friend Xavier. They used to get along really well but lately he was having a hard time. Xavier had been kind of rude and difficult to be around. He always wanted to do things his way and Montana was starting to feel like he wasn't a very good friend. He wanted to show Xavier how wrong he was and just go find a different friend to hang out with.

It's not always easy to be kind to each other. Sometimes it would be easier to insist on your own way or to focus on what you think you deserve. Thinking about what other people need takes practice and patience. When you remember how much God has forgiven you for, it makes it easier to stop looking at other people's faults. You have done plenty of things wrong, but God has been gracious to you. This is how you are supposed to treat others, with kindness and grace, remembering that neither of you deserve it.

Have you ever given up on someone
because of how they acted?

Created

We are God's creation. He created us to belong to Christ
Jesus. Now we can do good works. Long ago God
prepared these works for us to do.

Allan loved how being a Christian made him feel like he
belonged. He was blessed with a happy family, but he also
knew that following Jesus meant he was part of something
much bigger than his own family. He liked knowing he had
siblings all over the world, all doing their best to live in a way
that glorified God.

You are not an accident. You were created on purpose by
God. He made you to be part of his family. You are valuable
to him. No matter what your family looks like here on earth,
you have a glorious and loving family as a child of God. You
were created to glorify God and to reflect who he is. You are
a part of something much bigger than yourself. If you ever
feel lost or like you don't belong, remember you were created
to fit perfectly into God's family.

Does being part of God's family
change the way you feel about yourself?

Life

"The thief's purpose is to steal and kill and destroy.
My purpose is to give them a rich and satisfying life."
JOHN 10:10 NLT

Whenever something went wrong, Braxton felt like God
must be ignoring him. He must be busy taking care of
someone else's life because if he were paying attention to
Braxton then surely things would be easier. He thought
that if God really cared for him, he would make his life easy
and happy. If he really trusted God, then all of his problems
would disappear.

God wants your life to be rich and satisfying. He wants
you to experience his goodness. The truth is, his goodness
doesn't change when life gets hard. Even when you're walking
through something difficult, God can give you joy and keep
you steady. When the Bible talks about a rich and satisfying
life, it doesn't necessarily mean easy or simple. It means
you are depending on God and trusting in his goodness no
matter what. God doesn't want to take away all of the hard
things in life; he wants to help you walk through them.

Have you assumed if you trust God life will be easy?

Influence

Do not be fooled:
"Bad friends will ruin good habits."

1 CORINTHIANS 15:33 ICB

Mateo wanted to do the right thing, but it seemed like his friends were more interested in whatever made them laugh. After spending time with them, he often felt like he should apologize for the way he acted or the jokes he made. He just wanted to fit in, and it didn't seem like a big deal to say a few things he knew he shouldn't say. Mateo figured if they ever did anything really bad, he would just leave.

It is important to know how other people influence you. The people you surround yourself with can impact you in a positive or a negative way. The people you spend the most time with should cause you to be more like Jesus. They should encourage you in your relationship with him and help you to honor him in all you do. A good friend is one who makes you better, not worse. If your friends are causing you to make bad decisions, even small ones, then the difficult answer is probably that you need to spend less time with them.

What kind of influence do your closest friends
have on your life?

Clean

All who make themselves clean from evil will be used for special purposes. They will be made holy, useful to the Master, ready to do any good work.

2 TIMOTHY 2:21 NCV

Romeo thought he was doing all of the right things. He was reading his Bible, he was going to church, and he was even a leader in his youth group. He felt like he was being a good Christian, but if he was honest with himself his heart didn't feel right. He felt like he was doing all the right things on the outside but on the inside, he was a mess.

When the Bible talks about being clean, it isn't talking about how you look on the outside. God isn't concerned with what you look like. He is more concerned with what is happening in your heart. He sees past what everyone else sees. He knows your biggest worries and your most hidden thoughts. He doesn't just want you to do the right thing; he wants your heart to be clean and pure. The good news is he is the only one who can help you when your heart feels like a mess. He is strong enough to handle all of your mistakes and he loves to help his children.

What can you do when your heart
doesn't match your actions?

Lovable

Since God loved us that much,
we surely ought to love each other.

1 JOHN 4:11 NLT

Logan was really annoyed by the boy who sat next to him in class. They really didn't get along and Logan was frustrated by most of his actions. They weren't friends outside of class and so he didn't see why they needed to be friends in class. Couldn't Logan just focus on his schoolwork and ignore his classmate? Wouldn't that be okay as long as he wasn't mean?

Each person you encounter is lovable. No matter what faults or issues you see, each person is deserving of great love. You might look at someone and see the things you don't like or the things that bother you. No matter what your opinion is, God values each of his children. You aren't supposed to love others because of who they are; you are supposed to love them because of who God is. He loves you when you don't deserve it and so we are supposed to treat each other in that same way.

Is your love for others based on how you feel
about them or how God feels about them?

Growing

That will continue until we all become one in the faith.
We will also become one in the knowledge of God's Son.
Then we will be grown up in the faith.
We will receive everything that Christ has for us.

EPHESIANS 4:13 NIRV

Timothy really struggled on Sunday mornings. His class had been working on memorizing some Scripture and he was having a hard time. Memorization was difficult for him, and he felt like he was behind everyone else. He felt embarrassed that he didn't know as much as the other kids in the class. When he mentioned this to his teacher she kindly smiled and said, "Good thing we're all on the same team and it's not a competition. Don't be discouraged. God sees your efforts."

You are a work in progress. You have unique strengths and weaknesses that are part of who you are. You will spend the rest of your life growing in your faith. There will never be a point when you are done. This should be encouraging because it means that Christianity is not a competition of who can get to the end first. We are all on the same team, growing in our faith. Sometimes you will be the one succeeding and sometimes you will be the one struggling. We are all in this together.

Does knowing we are all growing in our faith
take some of the pressure off?

Alert

Pray in the Spirit at all times and on every occasion.
Stay alert and be persistent in your prayers
for all believers everywhere.

EPHESIANS 6:18 NLT

William felt like he should probably pray more. He knew
it was a good thing to do but he often felt like there were a
million other things asking for his attention. He wanted to
do what the Bible said and focus on God, but it was hard. He
wondered if God was disappointed in him. He felt like he
wasn't a very good Christian because he often forgot to pray.

The world is full of things that can distract you from what God
is doing. The Bible often talks about staying alert and paying
attention to what is going on. This is because God knows we
need to be reminded. He knows our weaknesses and he is
already aware of our lack of focus. He is not disappointed in
you, but he wants to help you. He doesn't tell you to pray more
because it's just a good thing to do. He knows that when you
pray, you will be encouraged and strengthened. Today, stay
alert and spend some time talking to God, not because you
have to, but because of his love for you.

Have you been viewing prayer as an item on a to-do list
or as a time to be encouraged by a God who loves you?

Peace

"I leave the gift of peace with you—my peace. Not the kind
of fragile peace given by the world, but my perfect peace.
Don't yield to fear or be troubled in your hearts—
instead, be courageous!"

JOHN 14:27 TPT

Frank stood with his family in church. The band was playing
a worship song he had never heard before and some of the
words caught his attention. It mentioned a peace that doesn't
make sense. He thought about this as his family sang around
him. He wanted to experience that kind of peace but wasn't
exactly sure what it meant.

Jesus wants to give you peace. He wants your heart to be
at rest. He doesn't want you to be anxious, worried, or
overwhelmed. The peace he gives you is supernatural and
perfect. He gives peace to his people when it doesn't make
sense. This means when everyone and everything around
you says you should be stressed out, Jesus wants to bless you
with peace so you aren't troubled. Even in the middle of a
storm, he can keep you safe and your heart can be quiet.

Have you been giving in to stress instead of
trusting the peace Jesus is offering?

Share

Don't forget to do good and to share with those in need.
These are the sacrifices that please God.

HEBREWS 13:16 NLT

Lincoln's Sunday school teacher had been talking about generosity, but he didn't really feel like he had much to give. He thought about his wallet at home and the dollar seventy-five that was inside of it. That wouldn't help anyone and so he didn't think the conversation about generosity applied to him at the moment. Maybe if he saved up his money he could think of a way to share some of it. When his teacher started talking about being generous with encouraging words and with your time, Lincoln realized he had thought about the whole topic in the wrong way.

There will always be someone who has more than you have, and there will always be someone who has less than you do. Sharing is not about keeping track of who has what or how much you can give. Instead, it's about having a generous spirit and being willing to share no matter what you have. Everything you have been given is a gift from God and sharing shows you trust him with what he has blessed you with. When you are generous with your time, money, words, and talents, it shows you are aware that God is the one who is in control.

In what area can you be generous where you had previously thought you didn't have enough to share?

Perfect

Christ suffered for our sins once for all time. He never
sinned, but he died for sinners to bring you safely home to
God. He suffered physical death, but he was raised to life in
the Spirit.

1 PETER 3:18 NLT

Morris loved a good hero story. He could get lost in the
pages of a book for hours at a time. He loved how there was
always someone to save the day. The hero always had exactly
what he needed to conquer the enemy. This was also what
he loved about Jesus. He was the perfect hero. The best part
was that he wasn't just a part of some story, he was real.
Everything he did actually happened and Morris loved being
part of it.

The perfection of Jesus is hard for us to even understand.
The very best thing we can experience on earth doesn't come
close to the perfection of Jesus. He was entirely perfect in
thought and in deed. This means that everything he said,
thought, and did was perfect. He didn't do anything wrong
ever. In all of his perfection, he chose to suffer for our sins.
He gave us a gift none of us deserve. He made a way for you
to be close to God.

How can you thank God today for
the perfect gift of Jesus?

Nourishing

"Anyone who eats my flesh and drinks my blood has eternal life, and I will raise that person at the last day."

JOHN 6:54 NLT

Paul sat in church with his parents. Everyone held a small cup of juice and a piece of bread in their hand. As the music played and the pastor talked about thanking Jesus for all he's done, Paul couldn't help but feel a little bit lost. He wasn't sure if he wanted to take communion and he wasn't really sure what the point was. How could a tiny cup and a bit of bread make any difference in his life anyway?

The elements of communion might be small, but the impact is large. If you are focused on the tiny cup and piece of bread, then you are missing the point. Communion is an opportunity to remember what Jesus has done for you. When you take the time to focus on the sacrifice he made for all of us, your faith is strengthened. It's so much more than a tradition we do sometimes at church. Every time you take communion, you turn your attention from yourself and what's happening around you, to who God is and the goodness of all he has done through Jesus.

Have you ever felt like communion was pointless? How can you change your perspective?

JUNE

"God is the one who saves me;
I will trust in him and not be afraid.
The LORD, the LORD gives me strength
and makes me sing.
He has saved me."

ISAIAH 12:2 NCV

Eternity

"Martha," Jesus said, "You don't have to wait until then.
I am the Resurrection, and I am Life Eternal. Anyone who
clings to me in faith, even though he dies, will live forever.
And the one who lives by believing in me will never die.
Do you believe this?"

JOHN 11:25-26 TPT

Colton loved counting down to his birthday. He'd mark the
days off on his calendar and watch the number get smaller
and smaller. It felt like it was an eternity to wait. In his mind,
a month or two was forever and it felt impossible to be
patient. It felt like forever, but he knew it actually wasn't. The
idea that something could really last forever was something
he couldn't wrap his mind around.

Your faith in Jesus means you will live forever. You will
spend eternity with God. This is part of the miracle of the
gospel. The idea of forever is something we don't even really
understand. Our minds can't make sense of something that
will never end. This should cause us to worship God even
more. He is so much wiser and stronger than we are. His
plans are better than we can ever understand.

Can you imagine how great eternity with Jesus will be?

Qualified

It is not that we think we are qualified to do anything
on our own. Our qualification comes from God.

2 CORINTHIANS 3:5 NLT

Jeremiah didn't always feel capable of being a good
Christian. He didn't feel like he had much to offer, and he
worried that he just wasn't good enough. When he shared
these thoughts with his youth leader, he reminded Jeremiah
he was valuable and needed. He told him he had everything
he needed because God promised he would provide for him.

If God has asked you to do something, he will equip you to
do it. He is the one who provides everything you need. Every
talent, skill, and resource you have comes from him. You are
qualified to do his will because of what he has already done
for you. You don't have to rely on whether or not you feel
good enough. God says you are good enough because you
have chosen to trust in him.

Have you been relying on your own skills or
on God's promises?

Ready

"You also must be ready. The Son of Man will come
at an hour when you don't expect him."

MATTHEW 24:44 NIRV

Oscar sat expectantly by the front window. His grandmother was coming to visit, and he was eager to see her. She lived really far away but whenever she made the trip to his house, she always came with a suitcase loaded full of surprises. He looked forward to seeing her with so much anticipation. While he waited for her, he had finished his homework, cleaned his room, and walked the dog. He didn't want anything to get in the way of his time with her.

No one knows exactly when Jesus will return. Together, we are all waiting and hoping for him to come back. Knowing he will make all things right makes his return exciting and worth waiting for. If you wait excitedly for a visit from a loved one now, imagine how great it will be when Jesus comes back. As you follow him now, you are getting ready for his return. As you spend time reading the Bible or learning about who God is, you are preparing for the day he comes back.

How can anticipating Jesus' return give you hope now?

Example

"I did this as an example so that
you should do as I have done for you."

JOHN 13:15 NCV

Jordan wandered around the yard with a group of second graders trailing behind him. It was his younger brother's birthday and he had agreed to help with the games. They were playing Follow the Leader. As he wove in and out of obstacles, he smiled and watched each partygoer try to keep their footing. No matter what he did, they tried their best to copy his actions.

If you are ever unsure of how to act or what to do, you can look at the way Jesus lived his life. In the New Testament you can see how he treated others and how he interacted with God. We know everything Jesus did reflected who God is. As you learn about who he was, and how he lived, you will know how to honor God and live a life that pleases him. Living a life that is glorifying to God is just like a game of Follow the Leader. Follow the example of Jesus and do as he did, and you'll be just fine.

Have you been following Jesus' example
or trying to make your own path?

Constant

Jesus Christ is the same yesterday and today and forever.

HEBREWS 13:8 NIRV

Magnus felt like everything around him was changing. He had friends who were moving away, and his family was switching churches. No matter how hard he tried, he felt like he couldn't get his footing. He felt uneasy, as though he just couldn't keep up. No matter how much changed, though, he did know he could rely on Jesus. His mom was constantly reminding him that Jesus never changes and he is good all of the time.

No matter what happens in the world, Jesus is steady. In the middle of tragedies like horrible storms or wars, Jesus is the same. In the middle of hard times, like sickness or depression, Jesus is the same. In the middle of everyday life, like dentist appointments or school attendance, Jesus is the same. He is always good, always patient, always loving, and always available. There is nothing you can do that can change who Jesus is. You can always rely on him.

Is there change happening in your life?
How can you rely on Jesus through it?

Treasures

"Don't store up treasures here on earth, where moths eat them and rust destroys them, and where thieves break in and steal. Store your treasures in heaven, where moths and rust cannot destroy, and thieves do not break in and steal."

MATTHEW 6:19-20 NLT

When Bennett thought about growing up, he mostly thought about independence. He was excited to go where he wanted, do what he wanted, and most of all, buy what he wanted. He imagined four wheelers, fishing gear, unlimited candy, and piles of video games. He loved to daydream about all of the stuff he would have.

What does it mean to store up treasures on earth? It means you are mainly focused on yourself and all you can have. When you just want more money, success, or fame, you will miss out on all God has to offer. Anything you gather on earth will not last but what you get from him will last forever. Focus on who he is and what he says, which is good. It's not bad to have things you enjoy, but those things are not supposed to be your best treasures.

What is something you can do today
to store up treasures in heaven?

Only

Serve only the LORD your God and fear him alone.
Obey his commands, listen to his voice, and cling to him.

DEUTERONOMY 13:4 NLT

Everett was trying to make his way through an obstacle course. He took a few steps forward but the blindfold covering his eyes kept him from knowing where to go. Everyone around him was shouting different directions and he couldn't figure out who to listen to. When he really focused, he could hear his partner's voice across the room telling him which way to go. If he ignored everyone else, he knew he would get to the end of the course safely.

Following God can be a lot like navigating an obstacle course. In your life, there will be many voices telling you what to do but it is important to listen only to God's voice. He is the one who will guide you and keep you safe. Stay close to him and follow his directions. Trust that he knows best and will be faithful to help you.

What can you do to help focus only on God's voice?

Give

Tell them to use their money to do good. They should be
rich in good works and generous to those in need,
always being ready to share with others.

1 TIMOTHY 6:18 NLT

Declan wandered into the garage where his older brother
was lifting weights. He watched him lift the heaviest ones
and decided he would try as well. He grabbed one and could
barely pick up. His brother smiled and said, "You've got to
start smaller than that; you're not strong enough yet."

The more you practice sharing, the better you will be at it.
It's like exercising a muscle until it gets as strong as you want
it to be. If you are lifting weights, you don't start with the
heaviest one. In the same way, it's okay to practice sharing
no matter how little you have. Ask God to help you to be
generous and you will learn how to give to others when you
have little or a lot.

What is one small way you can practice
being generous today?

Changed

Bodies made of flesh and blood can't share in the kingdom of God. And what dies can't share in what never dies. Listen! I am telling you a mystery. We will not all die. But we will all be changed. That will happen in a flash, as quickly as you can wink an eye. It will happen at the blast of the last trumpet.

1 CORINTHIANS 15:50-52 NIRV

Weston kept hearing his pastor talking about Jesus coming back. He talked about how the church would spend eternity with him. Weston knew he should be looking forward to that time, but he wasn't really sure why. When he asked his pastor about it, he told Weston to imagine perfection. He talked about how when Jesus returned, everything would be perfect.

Did you know when Jesus comes back, we will all be changed? He will make everything perfect again. The earth and everything in it will be exactly the way God meant for it to be. Your body will never be sick again and your relationships will all be perfect. There will be no more tears and no more pain. How exciting is it to think about how wonderful that will be?

Does thinking about how perfect everything will be make you feel excited for Jesus to come back?

Sympathy

All of you should be in agreement,
understanding each other, loving each other as family,
being kind and humble.

1 PETER 3:8 NCV

Ryder sat next to his best friend at school. He looked miserable. Without skipping a beat, Ryder said, "Man, I'm worried about the test too. Don't worry; you'll do fine." His friend looked at him a bit frustrated and said, "I don't care about the test. I'm frustrated about something else, which you would know if you had asked." Ryder realized that what he had assumed was wrong. He apologized and started asking a few question of his friend.

The Bible is full of reminders to be kind and peaceful towards other people. A big part of that is practicing being aware of how other people feel. It's important to remember there are parts of other people's lives you don't understand. It takes humility to realize you don't know everything. With humility, you can be sympathetic towards others and be gentle with their feelings and experiences.

Can you show the love of Jesus
by practicing being sympathetic today?

Suffer

In his kindness God called you to share in his eternal glory
by means of Christ Jesus. So after you have suffered a little
while, he will restore, support, and strengthen you,
and he will place you on a firm foundation.

1 PETER 5:10 NLT

Sawyer knew his parents were going through a difficult time.
He didn't know all of the details, but they seemed really sad
and stressed out. One day, he asked his mom if everything
was going to be okay. She smiled at him and said, "We can
walk through incredibly difficult days because we know what
is coming. We are motivated by knowing Jesus will come
back, not by how easy our life is." He felt encouraged by her
words and really thought about what they meant.

We will all experience suffering at some point. Life can be
painful, and we don't always have control over the hard
things that happen. The wonderful thing about following
Jesus is you know that pain won't last forever. One day Jesus
will fix everything and make it all right. You can have great
hope because he will always keep his promises. Instead of
focusing on what is hard, you can focus on what is coming.

When you experience suffering are you discouraged,
or do you hope in Jesus?

Power

We now have this light shining in our hearts, but we
ourselves are like fragile clay jars containing this great
treasure. This makes it clear that our great power
is from God, not from ourselves.

2 CORINTHIANS 4:7 NLT

Victor had always felt pressure to be perfect. He liked doing
everything right and he felt good about himself when he
succeeded. When he unexpectedly got a bad grade on a test,
he was miserable. When he talked with his mom about it,
she reminded him that only God is perfect and our mistakes
can remind us to worship him.

Christianity is not about what people can do, but what God
can do with people. If you pay attention, you will quickly see
that people make mistakes and are full of flaws. It is clear
that no one is perfect. This doesn't mean you should focus on
those flaws. Instead, when people mess up it should remind
you that perfection belongs only to God. He is the only one
can do no wrong. His power is made perfect in
our weakness.

How do your faults glorify God?

Sacrifice

We see Jesus, who as a man, lived for a short time lower than the angels and has now been crowned with glorious honor because of what he suffered in his death. For it was by God's grace that he experienced death's bitterness on behalf of everyone! For now he towers above all creation, for all things exist through him and for him.

HEBREWS 2:9-10 TPT

For maybe the first time in his life, Winston felt astonished by what Jesus had done for him. He saw the sacrifice that was made for him, and it made him want to follow Jesus for all of his days. He felt loved and taken care of in a way he hadn't before. He felt like his eyes had been opened to a truth he hadn't understood before.

Jesus sacrificed everything in order to bring us to God. When he came to earth as a baby, he left perfection. He gave up his heavenly position and came to earth to be mocked and killed. His sacrifice is the reason you have salvation. Your sins are wiped clean because of what he did. You can honor that sacrifice.

If you haven't grasped Jesus' sacrifice before, how can you renew your faith?

Listen

My dear brothers, always be willing to listen
and slow to speak. Do not become angry easily.

JAMES 1:19 ICB

Zachary stubbornly held his tongue. He kept his mouth
shut and tried his hardest to listen to his sister who was
explaining why she was frustrated. All he wanted to do was
shout his opinion at her and argue his case. Instead, he was
determined to listen closely to what she had to say. As he
remained silent, he felt his anger begin to melt away. They
talked about their argument and Zachary felt so proud he
hadn't exploded.

Being willing to listen to others shows a lot of maturity. It's
not easy to keep your mouth shut when your emotions are
bubbling over. It takes a lot of self-control to speak calmly
when you're upset. The Bible mentions several times the
power of a quiet tongue. God knows we need to be reminded
often. If you struggle with listening to others, ask God to
have mercy on you and to help you where you are weak.

What is something you can do
to practice listening today?

Dance

Break forth with dancing!
Make music and sing God's praises
with the rhythm of the drums!

PSALM 149:3 TPT

Kieran had always been a pretty serious rule follower. He had spent so much time worrying about being a good Christian he had forgotten the joy that comes with salvation. He was so worried about checking things off of his list and following all of the right rules he didn't leave any room for celebration. It didn't even occur to him that God would want to see him full of delight.

Christianity is not just a long list of rules to follow. It's not all about solemnly thinking about death or suffering or sins. Christianity is also meant to be a great celebration! God is full of joy, and he wants to see you live a joyful life as well. He has given us an endless list of things to be glad about. You can celebrate who he is and what he has done in any way you like. You can dance, you can sing, you can shout. Your celebration honors him just as much as your obedience.

How can you joyfully celebrate today
in a way that honors God?

Amazing

In the middle of them was someone who looked like a son of man. He was dressed in a long robe with a gold strip of cloth around his chest. The hair on his head was white like wool, as white as snow. His eyes were like a blazing fire. His feet were like bronze metal glowing in a furnace. His voice sounded like rushing waters.

REVELATION 1:13-15 NIRV

Chase had never met his Uncle Jim. He lived in another country and traveling had been difficult for their family to figure out. This summer for the first time, they would be going to visit him. Chase was so excited to get to know him. He had heard stories about him and in some ways, he felt like he knew him already. He couldn't wait to see him in person and to spend time with him.

It can be hard to understand what someone really looks like until you've met them face-to-face. When you think about Jesus, you might have a picture in your mind, but one day you will see him right in front of you. One day you won't have to imagine any more what he looks like or sounds like. That day will be amazing and exciting! We can read about what he is like in the Bible and that can help but think about how incredible it will be to see him with your own eyes.

What is one thing you are looking forward to doing when you see Jesus face-to-face?

Watchful

Be alert. Continue strong in the faith.
Have courage, and be strong.
Do everything in love.

1 CORINTHIANS 16:13-14 NCV

John and his family were just starting their annual camping trip. His parents were busy putting up the tent and he asked if he could wander around the campground for a bit. His mom said it was fine as long as he stayed alert and watchful. As he walked away from their site, he paid attention to what he saw and where he went. He wanted to be able to get back without any problems.

As a Christian, it is important to be watchful. You need to pay attention to what is going on around you and how that impacts the choices you make. Life will be full of opportunities to either honor God or to forget your faith. Just like you are alert when you're in a new place, be alert in life as you do your best to follow Jesus.

How does being alert help you to follow Jesus?

Known

"I knew you before I formed you in your mother's womb.
Before you were born I set you apart
and appointed you as my prophet to the nations."

JEREMIAH 1:5 NLT

Christopher sat at his desk and tried his best to come up with some good ideas. He was working on a school assignment and felt completely stuck. He was supposed to write an essay about who he was. He had written down all of the main points and he still only had a paragraph. It was harder than he thought it would be to explain himself to others.

You are completely known by God. There is not a single part of you that is a mistake or a mystery. He sees and understands all of you. Whenever you feel frustrated or misunderstood, you can trust that God always understands. You can talk to him and be confident he knows your heart. He knows you better than you know yourself. He is your creator and knows every little thing about you.

Does being fully known by God make you
feel loved and comfortable?

Persistent

Rejoice in our confident hope.
Be patient in trouble, and keep on praying.

ROMANS 12:12 NLT

Edward had joined the cross-country team and his end-of-the-year meet was coming up. He had trained all year for this run. It was the longest one he'd ever done, and he had worked really hard. Each time they practiced his coach reminded him how important it was not to quit. "You can run further than you think you can," he would say. "Keep your focus on the end goal and you will find that each small step adds up to an entire race."

Don't give up! You don't need to be a good Christian for a week, or a month, or even five years. The goal is to follow Jesus for all of your days. A lot of Christianity is about developing perseverance. This is the ability to be persistent in your pursuit of Jesus no matter what. Christianity is not a sprint; it is a marathon. No matter what happens, keep your focus on who Jesus is and what he is doing. Trust that he will one day make all things right.

When you feel like quitting, what can you do to stay persistent in your relationship with Jesus?

Prize

I do not mean that I am already as God wants me to be.
I have not yet reached that goal. But I continue trying to
reach it and to make it mine. Christ wants me to do that.
That is the reason Christ made me his. Brothers, I know that
I have not yet reached that goal. But there is one thing
I always do: I forget the things that are past. I try as hard
as I can to reach the goal that is before me.

PHILIPPIANS 3:12-13 ICB

Florian laughed at his little brother. He was helping his
mom in the yard and she had promised him a penny for
every weed he pulled. Even though the prize was silly, the
little boy worked eagerly and excitedly. He couldn't wait for
his reward. It didn't matter how dirty his hands got, or how
stubborn a weed was. He worked steadily because he only
had one goal in mind: putting those pennies in his pocket.
The prize motivated him.

As you follow Jesus, the prize you are working for is eternity
with God. When life gets difficult remember one day Jesus
will come back and make everything right. It seems long, but
your life is actually very short in comparison to the eternity
you will spend with God. Your goal is to live with him
forever. What you do now impacts your life in eternity.

When you face a trial, how can you keep
your focus on the prize of eternity with Jesus?

Offering

Since God has shown us great mercy, I beg you to offer your
lives as a living sacrifice to him. Your offering must
be only for God and pleasing to him.

ROMANS 12:1 NCV

Tripp was so excited to play with his new soccer ball. He
and a friend were kicking it around on a Saturday afternoon.
He ran up to it and sent it flying with all of his might. It
shot towards the top of his neighbor's fence. This particular
neighbor really hated when their toys ended up in his yard
and he had warned that the next time it happened, he
wouldn't return it. His friend stopped it just in time. "Oh
man, I owe you one," he said gratefully.

Even in small ways like with a soccer ball, we understand
that when someone does something kind, it is nice to return
the favor. God has done great things for you. He sent his
only son to die so your sins would be wiped clean. He is
merciful toward you when you don't deserve it. We offer
our lives to him because we know without him, we would
have nothing. When you are obedient to him it shows that
you understand all he has done for you. When you serve
him joyfully you acknowledge that his great love is what has
saved you from your sins.

Have you thought lately about
all that God has done for you?

Wise

Listen to me and you will be prudent and wise.
For even the foolish and feeble can receive an understanding
heart that will change their inner being.

PROVERBS 8:5 TPT

Avery didn't know how to handle the situation he was in.
He had been invited to multiple activities over the weekend
and he was really struggling to decide. His mom told him
to use wisdom because his time was valuable. This felt
overwhelming to Avery, and he wasn't sure how to go about
making the right choice. He certainly didn't feel very wise
and wasn't sure what to do.

Wisdom means having good judgement and knowing how
to apply truth to your life. The Bible says we should seek
wisdom and eagerly desire it. The good news is that wisdom
has nothing to do with intelligence or natural skill. If you are
not wise, you don't need to feel inadequate. God says you can
ask him for wisdom, and he will give it to you. He loves to
give wisdom to his children.

Have you ever asked God for wisdom?

Repent

Repent of your sins and turn to God, so that your sins may
be wiped away. Then times of refreshment will come from
the presence of the Lord, and he will again send you Jesus,
your appointed Messiah.

ACTS 3:19-20 NLT

Let's imagine Jeremy got into a big fight with his sister. He
ended up calling her some pretty mean names. At the end
of the day, he went to apologize for his actions but instead
of talking to her, he apologized to his brother. That doesn't
make sense, does it? The apology only works if you talk to
the right person.

The same is true about God. He is the only one who can
forgive your sins. It doesn't make sense to leave him out of
it. None of your mistakes are big enough to keep you from
God. When you ask him for forgiveness, he is always waiting
for you, ready to wipe your sins away. He wants you to run to
him, knowing he is the one who will refresh you. When you
make mistakes, don't be afraid or embarrassed to talk to God
about it. He is the only one who can truly bring you freedom
and help you repent.

Have you ever been afraid to
talk to God about your mistakes?

Relevant

All Scripture is inspired by God and is useful for teaching,
for showing people what is wrong in their lives, for
correcting faults, and for teaching how to live right.

2 TIMOTHY 3:16 NCV

Gideon knew he should probably read his Bible. Years of
being taught about God's Word meant he knew he would be
encouraged if he read it. At the same time, he also felt like
most of the Bible was boring and he didn't understand how
it applied to his life. Wasn't it just full of stories he had
already learned?

You might know a lot about what is in the Bible, or you
might barely be familiar with it. No matter what amount of
knowledge you have, it's important to understand the Bible
is always relevant. This means it always applies. There will
never be a time when you can stop learning from God's
Word. His Word is a wonderful gift and a great teaching tool.
Reading it can help you to live a life that pleases God. If you
find his Word boring, ask him to help you to read it in a way
that makes it come alive.

Have you ever skipped over reading your Bible
because you thought it was boring?

Friendship

"I don't call you servants now. A servant does not know what his master is doing. But now I call you friends because I have made known to you everything I heard from my Father."

JOHN 15:15 ICB

Dillon sat with his brother watching a basketball game. His favorite player made the winning shot and for the next few minutes they talked about how cool he was. "Wouldn't it be great to get to play with him?" Dillon asked his brother. "Yeah right," he answered. "Like someone that great would ever be your friend."

Have you ever imagined being friends with someone greater, more talented, or richer than you are? It seems like a crazy dream, right? The Creator of the entire universe calls you his friend. He is more powerful than anyone or anything you can imagine. He is more perfect than we will ever understand. He is stronger, richer, greater, wiser, and more beautiful than you can grasp, and he still calls you his friend. The way God interacts with us is incredible. He doesn't call you a servant, a simple creation, or a slave. He says you are the most important thing in the universe to him. You are his child, his friend, and his treasure.

How does thinking about God as your friend change how you approach him?

Glorious

On the glorious splendor of your majesty,
and on your wondrous works, I will meditate.

PSALM 145:5 NLT

Garrett walked around outside. He was kind of distracted but was trying his best to focus on God. His Bible study teacher had suggested they go for a prayer walk this week and take some time to appreciate God's glory. He had explained this simply meant talking to God while you enjoy some time outside. Garrett thought this was a good idea, but he honestly didn't know what it meant to focus on the glory of God.

God is glorious. This means he has striking beauty and splendor. He is worthy of fame and admiration. When you know God is glorious, you will worship and adore him. If you are unsure of what that means, ask God to show you. Anytime there is something about God you don't see or understand, you can ask for his help. He will be faithful to show you.

Did you know you can ask God
to show you how to worship?

Obedient

As you deal with one another, you should think and act as Jesus did. In his very nature he was God. Jesus was equal with God. But Jesus didn't take advantage of that fact. Instead, he made himself nothing. He did this by taking on the nature of a servant. He was made just like human beings. He appeared as a man. He was humble and obeyed God completely. He did this even though it led to his death.

PHILIPPIANS 2:5-8 NIRV

Tyson wanted to be obedient to God but sometimes it seemed overwhelming. He wasn't always sure what to do. Even when he tried to make the right choices, he often felt like he was in over his head. When he shared this with his dad, he reminded Tyson that he didn't need to be overwhelmed. "Good thing you have an example to follow," he said to his son.

If you don't understand what it means to be obedient to God, you can always look at how Jesus lived. Everything he did was perfect, and the Bible says that he obeyed God completely. If you try to live in a way that reflects what Jesus did, that will result in you being obedient to God. You can ask the Holy Spirit to help you follow Jesus' example in the things you say, the thoughts you think, and the way you go about your day.

How can you follow Jesus' example today?

Dependent

The LORD is good to those who depend on him,
   to those who search for him.
   So it is good to wait quietly
   for salvation from the LORD.
LAMENTATIONS 3:25-26 NLT

Asher's family was moving to a different house. Everything they owned was being packed into boxes as they approached moving day. His little brother had never moved before, and he was very concerned that his favorite things wouldn't make it to the new house. Asher wasn't worried. He knew his mom and dad had it under control. They were capable of handling everything well. He knew he could depend on them.

What does it mean to depend on God? When you depend on someone it means you trust them, or you rely on them. For example, if your family were moving, you would depend on your parents to get you and your belongings safely to the new house. When you depend on God you are counting on him to do what he says he will do. You are believing he will be true to his Word and will keep his promises. You aren't worried or anxious because you are trusting in his care.

Have you been worried about something in your life instead of depending on God to handle it?

Judge

Whenever the LORD raised up a judge over Israel, he was with that judge and rescued the people from their enemies throughout the judge's lifetime. For the LORD took pity on his people, who were burdened by oppression and suffering.

JUDGES 2:18 NLT

Jax noticed a lot of people were talking about the government lately. People seemed frustrated and annoyed that things were not happening like they wanted. They were discussing it as a family around the dinner table when his parents explained that no matter who is at the top of the government, God's throne is still higher. No one can take away his position or authority.

God can help his people no matter who is leading them. No matter who is in charge of a country, God is the one who is in control of the whole earth. He is the King of kings and the Lord of lords. He is the true judge of all. Even if things are happening in the world that don't make sense, we can still trust that God is powerful enough to make sure his will is done. He will always be faithful to his people.

Is your trust in the authority of people or the authority of God?

Inheritance

It is by his great mercy that we have been born again. Now we live with great expectation, and we have a priceless inheritance—an inheritance that is kept in heaven for you, pure and undefiled, beyond the reach of change and decay.

1 PETER 1:4 NLT

Rick's dad was a farmer. He owned a large ranch and they raised cattle for beef. The farm used to belong to his grandfather. Before that it belonged to his great-grandfather. The same land had been in his family for over a hundred years. It had been passed down from one person to the next and one day it would probably be Rick's. Being part of Rick's family meant inheriting that farm.

Inheritance is a word you might not hear very often. An inheritance is something that is passed down from one person to another. Often when someone passes away, their belongings or wealth is inherited by their children or by other members of their family. Just like you might inherit land from your parents, as part of God's family you get to inherit all he has. You are his beloved child, and he has not left you empty-handed. He has given you the greatest gift: salvation and security in Jesus.

Does knowing you have an inheritance make you feel part of God's family?

JULY

He gives strength
to those who are tired
and more power
to those who are weak.

ISAIAH 40:29 NCV

Justified

Since we have been made right with God by our faith,
we have peace with God.
This happened through our Lord Jesus Christ.

ROMANS 5:1 NCV

Keith had not grown up going to church. He was the first
person in his family to follow Jesus and he felt like he had so
much to learn. He would go to church on Sunday morning with
his neighbor and every week he learned something new. He
had never understood words like justification, righteousness, or
sanctification. These felt like big concepts, but he was learning
that they were the building blocks of his faith.

Being justified before God means you are in right standing
with him. God is so perfect that we shouldn't even be able
to be near him because of our own imperfections. You
are justified because of what Jesus did on the cross. You
can approach God and be near to him because of Christ's
sacrifice. He has made you perfect and wiped your sins clean
so you can know God.

Have you ever thought about
what it means to be justified?

Faithful

All the LORD's ways are loving and faithful
toward those who obey what his covenant commands.

PSALM 25:10 NIRV

Michael ran steadily down the soccer field. As he moved
toward the ball, he heard his parents cheering his name.
He loved having them at his games. They were always
encouraging and kind. He knew they were his biggest fans.
Knowing they were proud of him make him feel loved and
cared for. Their excitement encouraged him to do his best.

God is faithful. This means he doesn't quit. He is loyal and
kind. He is on your side, and he wants to guide you through
your days. He is not looking down at you, waiting for you
to mess up or make mistakes. He is with you, ready to
encourage you and help you in whatever way you need. He is
proud of you and is happy you are his son. Just like a parent
cheering you on at a soccer game, God is cheering you on in
life. His pride in you can motivate you to follow him.

Have you felt like God is disappointed in you or have
you been encouraged by how proud he is of you?

Result

You have been set free from sin.
God has made you his slaves.
The benefit you gain leads to holy living.
And the end result is eternal life.

ROMANS 6:22 NIRV

Sean finished taking out the trash and went to find his older brother. He had said if Sean did his chores, he would take him out for ice cream. Now that he was done, he was excited about the outing. The only problem was his brother was nowhere to be found. Sean felt frustrated and tricked. He had done the work and he wanted the reward that he was promised.

When you spend your life following Jesus, it isn't for nothing. He doesn't ask you to do the right thing and then refuse to reward you. He isn't hiding from you or far away when you need him. He will keep his promises and stay true to his Word. The great reward is you get to spend eternity with God. The result of you trusting God is you get to be with him forever.

Do you believe God will keep his promises to you?

Freedom

Let me be clear, the Anointed One has set us free—not partially, but completely and wonderfully free! We must always cherish this truth and stubbornly refuse to go back into the bondage of our past.

GALATIANS 5:1 TPT

Basil loved watching funny videos with his dad. They were sitting on the couch watching a clip of a group of people trying to help a sheep. The animal had walked into a small ditch and gotten stuck. They got him free, then he ran a few feet and immediately jumped back into the ditch. It was so funny! This happened twice before the sheep finally ran in the other direction. He and his dad laughed and laughed.

You have been set free from sin! Don't wander back into a place where you were enslaved. It's a funny way of looking at it but when you forget about your freedom, it's just like the sheep who was rescued and immediately jumped back into entrapment. When we go back into the bondage of our past, it's like saying that what Jesus did on the cross wasn't enough. Everyday remember he has died so you may be free.

Have you thanked God for your freedom lately?

Grit

How much longer must I cling to this constant grief?
I've endured this shaking of my soul.
So how much longer will my enemy have the upper hand?
It's been long enough!

PSALM 13:2 TPT

Cruz was picking weeds in his mom's garden on a Saturday morning. He had thirty minutes left of chores before he was allowed to play video games. He was faced with a dilemma. He knew what he should do but it wasn't what he wanted to do. He wanted to slow down and maybe just make it look like he was doing a good job. He didn't feel like working hard for another thirty minutes. Besides, he didn't think his mom would even notice if he slowed down.

Following Jesus takes grit and endurance. Sometimes you will be tempted to give up. It's not always easy or comfortable to do the right thing. In those moments, it's up to you to decide if you will persevere or not. No one else can make that choice for you. There will be times in your life when you have to decide what path to take. When you need it, God will give you the grace to make the right choices. Ask him for endurance and he will help you.

When you give up early,
who does that negatively impact?

Happy

I realize that the best thing for them is to be happy and enjoy themselves as long as they live. God wants all people to eat and drink and be happy in their work, which are gifts from God.

ECCLESIASTES 3:12-13 NCV

Lazlo had his first summer job this year. He was mowing lawns in his neighborhood, and he was enjoying having extra spending money. He liked being outside and meeting people he had never met before. At first, he spent his money on some candy. Then he saved up for a video game. Then he decided to save up for a new skateboard. it seemed like the more he bought, the more he wanted. By the end of the summer, he grew tired of mowing lawns and just wanted the money without the work. As he focused on what he could buy, he lost the happiness that the actual job had brought him.

God wants you to enjoy your life. He himself is full of joy and he wants you to experience that joy. That doesn't mean your life will always be easy or simple. But it does mean he wants you to have a happiness that comes from the inside. When your joy comes from God, it doesn't matter what material things you have or what your life looks like on the outside. When your greatest happiness comes from God, your days will be full of joy as well.

Has your happiness come from God
or from the things you have?

Sing

Sing to him. Sing praise to him.
Tell about all the wonderful things he has done.

1 CHRONICLES 16:9 NIRV

Egan sat in church with his family. The worship leader had just told everyone they could sing their own songs to the Lord. As he heard different voices rise up around him, Egan couldn't help but feel unsure about what to say. He didn't know the right words and he didn't think his voice was very nice. He didn't want to do the wrong thing.

When you sing praises to the Lord, they don't have to make sense to anyone else but you. You don't have to have a perfect voice or the perfect song. Just say whatever is on your mind. He is paying attention to you and your words are important to him. He knows your heart and he isn't worried about you singing the exact right thing. Worship can be messy and that's okay. Praise him for who he is and what he has done for you.

Has your worship been about telling God what's on your heart or making sure you say just the right thing?

Develop

We can rejoice, too, when we run into problems and trials, for we know that they help us develop endurance. And endurance develops strength of character, and character strengthens our confident hope of salvation.

ROMANS 5:3-4 NLT

Ari ran until his lungs burned and his legs couldn't go any further. He was training for a cross country meet. No matter how hard one day of running was, he knew it was getting him closer to his goal. He knew with each step his muscles were getting stronger, and his body was developing endurance. Every single practice, no matter how it went, was preparing him for his race.

It's easy to get frustrated when things don't go the way you want. It can be discouraging, and you might feel tired of problems. It's normal to feel that way, but the Bible tells us that trials can actually be a good thing. This is because they help you to develop endurance. This means when you face something difficult, it makes you stronger for the next trial. It's just like training for a race. Each practice makes you better and better. Life will have ups and downs. That cannot be avoided. But you can control the attitude you have about it.

When you know a trial is helping you develop endurance, does that make it easier to deal with?

Work

Lazy people want much but get little,
but those who work hard will prosper.

PROVERBS 13:4 NLT

In the summer, Adan spent the first part of each Saturday helping his dad in the yard. This week it was particularly hot and as he finished mowing the grass, sweat dripped down his forehead. He was tired, but the thought of jumping in the pool when he was done kept him going. That feeling of plunging into the cool water was made even better by how hard he was working.

God designed us to need rest. Rest is good and wonderful. We aren't supposed to be exhausted or constantly stressed out. Rest is needed to be able to recharge and also to make sure we are focused on God and not just on our work. It's important you learn how to balance rest and work. One is not more important than the other. When you work hard, rest is sweet. When you are lazy, rest can't be enjoyed the way God intended.

Do you have a balance of rest and work in your life or are you too focused on one side or the other?

Teach

I am sure that you are full of goodness.
I know that you have all the knowledge you need
and that you are able to teach each other.

ROMANS 15:14 ICB

Sebastian really loved going to youth group. Each
Wednesday he got to spend a few hours with some of his
closest friends, playing games and learning about Jesus.
His youth leader was one of his favorite people. Sebastian
liked him because he talked them about God and his Word,
but more importantly, he made each person feel loved and
valued. He didn't just tell them how they should live, he
showed them.

The way you live can teach other people about who Jesus
is. When you follow his example, then what you do will
reflect who he is. It is important to use your words to talk
about what God has done, but it is equally important to
teach others by using your actions. The way you treat others
should show them how much God loves them. Without
actions, your words are empty.

What about how you live would persuade
someone to learn about Jesus?

Ponder

Continue to think about the things that are good and worthy of praise. Think about the things that are true and honorable and right and pure and beautiful and respected.

PHILIPPIANS 4:8 ICB

Jeff was usually a pretty positive person. This is why it really surprised him when he woke up one Saturday and just felt crummy. It seemed like everything that went through his head was negative and wrong. He couldn't seem to stop thinking things he didn't want to think. His mom could see he was struggling so she offered to help. They went on a walk and listened to some worship music. She prayed with him and suggested he try to refocus.

The things you ponder will be the things that define your life. Your thoughts are important. They might be hidden from everyone around you, but they have the power to impact every aspect of your life. You can't always control what you think, but you can practice the discipline of taking your thoughts captive. As you train your mind, you'll learn to focus on what is good.

If you have a day full of thoughts you don't like, what can you do to refocus?

True

Love must be honest and true.
Hate what is evil.
Hold on to what is good.

ROMANS 12:9 NIV

Ewan came home from school to find out that his dog was acting kind of funny. She was curled up in the corner and his mom said she hadn't eaten or drank any water all day. She seemed to be in pain, and they were getting worried about her. His mom decided it was time to act, so she called the vet. They loaded their dog into the car and drove to the clinic hoping they could get some answers.

If you want to understand why your dog is sick, you'd talk to a vet. If you wanted to understand how to do your math homework, you would talk to your teacher. It only makes sense to find the expert on the subject in which you need help. In the same way, if you want to understand true love, then you need to get to know who God is. God is love. Everything about him is loving. It's his nature. He cannot do anything that is unloving. He is the expert and the only one who can teach you what is good and right.

What do you think will happen if you try
to understand true love without God?

Learn

Do what you learned and received from me,
what I told you, and what you saw me do.
And the God who gives peace will be with you.

PHILIPPIANS 4:9 NCV

Scout loved his grandfather. He had learned a lot from him.
He taught Scout how to fish, how to carve little toys out of
pieces of wood, and how to build a campfire all by himself.
His grandfather loved being outside, and he passed a lot of
his skills onto Scout. But he didn't just teach him how to
do those things, he taught him how to be kind, patient, and
generous to everyone he met. Scout learned valuable skills
and qualities from him.

Sometimes God puts people in your life to teach you
something. He knows what you need to learn, and he will
provide you with the right teachers. It's important to follow
good examples and be a good student in life. There are people
in your life who can teach you about who God is and how to
honor him. Listen to them and hear what they have to say.

Who has God put in your life
to teach you about who he is?

Support

Insult your Creator, will you? That's exactly what you do every time that you oppress the powerless! Showing kindness to the poor is equal to honoring your maker.

PROVERBS 14:31 TPT

Bryan walked through the hallway at school. He noticed another boy dropped some of his books and was trying to pick them up. The bell had already rung and everyone was rushing to class. Not a single person stopped to help the boy on the floor. When Bryan walked over and picked up a book, the boy thanked him as though he had never been helped in his life. It was like that small action made his entire day. Bryan thought about how easy it would have been to walk past him and was glad he had stopped to help.

Being a Christian isn't just about knowing who Jesus is and understanding the Bible. If you want to live a life that honors God, then you must treat other people the way he would treat them. You can't just read about God. Your faith must impact your actions as well. The Bible says that when you support others and show kindness, you are honoring God. Love the people whom others look past. Lift up and encourage the lonely. This is pleasing to God.

Do you notice when others need help? Ask God to open your eyes to see when people are in need.

Royalty

"You have made them members of a royal family.
You have made them priests to serve our God.
They will rule on the earth."

REVELATION 5:10 NIRV

Teddy sat at the dinner table and looked around at his family. He knew he was lucky. His family was big, loud, and full of love. He knew he belonged and was part of something wonderful. He was proud to be a member of his family. He was thankful for the family he was given. Even on his worst day, his siblings and his parents made him feel like everything would be okay.

If you ever feel like you don't belong, remember who your Father is. Remember you are royalty. You are part of a family and that means you will never be alone. No matter what your earthly family is like, you are part of something wonderful. Because of what Jesus did on the cross, you have been adopted into the royal family of God. You are a son of the King. Let that truth make you feel loved, wanted, and cherished.

How does being part of a royal family make you feel?

Valuable

I called out to the LORD.
He is worthy of praise.
He saved me from my enemies.

PSALM 18:3 NIRV

Brett wandered through his neighborhood with his dad. It was Saturday morning and a lot of people on his block were having yard sales. They stopped at one house and his dad saw an old bike so he went to talk to the owner. "How much do you want for that bike?" he asked. The man replied he wanted fifty dollars. Brett's dad bought the bike and they started walking it home. When Brett asked why he bought it, his dad explained that it was an antique and it was actually worth a lot more than that. The fifty dollars was a small price for what he was getting in return.

In the same way, God's worth is far greater than what you have to offer him. You give him your praise, and what you get in return is eternity with him. God is worth all of your praise. He is wiser, stronger, and more kind than we can ever understand. You will never encounter anyone on the earth who is as great as God is. Everything about him is worthy of your praise.

What can you do today to praise God?

Welcome

Remember to welcome strangers, because some who have
done this have welcomed angels without knowing it.

HEBREWS 13:2 NCV

Trevor sat on the bus and watched a new student walk down
the aisle between the seats. Most of the seats he passed had
space for him, but no one moved over to allow him to sit
down. When he got closer, Trevor motioned he could sit
with him. They talked during the ride to school and Trevor
learned that this boy had just moved to town. His grandma
was very sick, and they had moved in order to be closer to
her. Trevor was glad he had been kind to him; it seemed like
he really needed it.

Every single person who you meet is loved and cherished by
God. It is important that you treat everyone with dignity and
respect. You have no way of knowing what someone else's life
is like or what they've been through. This is why it is important
to welcome everyone with kindness and patience. The way you
treat people teaches them about how God loves them.

How can you practice welcoming strangers
and being kind to everyone?

Secret

"The time is coming when everything that is covered up will be revealed, and all that is secret will be made known to all."

LUKE 12:2 NLT

Arvin followed his family through the halls of a museum. They were on vacation, and they were taking a tour to look at some pieces of art that his mom was interested in. He had no idea where they were going but their tour guide was confident. He knew the ins and outs of every room, who painted what, and how each piece came to be in that museum. He was knowledgeable and made Arvin feel comfortable even though he had never been there before.

God is full of wisdom and knowledge, and he is helping you through each day. It's like having the best tour guide ever. He knows everything and is on your side. He knows exactly how many mistakes you will make, and he still never gives up on you. You cannot keep secrets from God. This shouldn't make you feel like you are being watched over by a ruler who is just waiting for you to mess up. Instead, it should make you feel free and safe.

Does knowing that nothing is a secret give you confidence in God's leadership?

Present

"Anyone who wants to serve me must follow me,
because my servants must be where I am.
And the Father will honor anyone who serves me."

JOHN 12:26 NLT

Dolton sat in Sunday school and was thinking about his relationship with God. After listening to the lesson, he started to realize the only time he really thought about God was on Sundays at church. He wanted to have a relationship with him, and he was learning in order to do that, he would need to spend time with him.

If you want to follow Jesus, you need to be present with him. You can't follow him without being close to him. You can practice being in the presence of God. At first, spending time with him might seem strange or weird but the more you do it, the more natural it will feel. To spend time with him you can pray, sing songs of worship, and read your Bible. You can enjoy his creation and ask him to teach you about who he is. There are many ways to be with God.

What can you do today to be close to God?

Fullness

We pray that you would walk in the ways of true righteousness, pleasing God in every good thing you do. Then you'll become fruit-bearing branches, yielding to his life, and maturing in the rich experience of knowing God in his fullness!

COLOSSIANS 1:10 TPT

Garret asked his grandmother for a cookie. When he was done eating it, he asked her for another one. And another. And another. At home, he would never ask that many times because he knew his mom would say no. But when it came to cookies at Grandma's house, the rules were different. He knew he could ask almost as many times as he wanted, and she would always say yes.

In the same way, you can always ask God to know him more because you can be confident he will always say yes. God has no limits, and he wants you to experience the fullness of who he is. This means he wants you to know all of him. He doesn't want you to just know him a little bit or in part. Don't be satisfied with just experiencing God in a small way. Always be asking for more. He will never run out of love, wisdom, or grace to give to you.

Have you limited your relationship with God, or have you been asking for more?

Passion

Be enthusiastic to serve the Lord, keeping your passion
toward him boiling hot! Radiate with the glow of the Holy
Spirit and let him fill you with excitement as you serve him.

ROMANS 12:11 TPT

Gaston dragged his feet. He was supposed to be cleaning his
room, but he really didn't want to. He slowly moved from
item to item, getting distracted along the way. The actual job
wasn't very hard, but he didn't feel like doing it. He wasn't
very motivated and so it was taking him a lot longer to do
than it should have. By the time he was done, half the day
was gone.

Have you ever tried to do something you just weren't excited
about? It's harder, isn't it? Sometimes, it takes more energy
to work up the motivation to do the task than to actually
just do it. Following Jesus isn't supposed to be like that.
He doesn't want you to feel frustrated or bored in your
relationship with him. He wants you to feel excited and
enthusiastic to serve God. If you don't feel that way, the
answer is simple. Ask God to change your heart! Ask for
help and he will give it to you. When you have the passion,
serving God is a delight.

Are you passionate about serving God today?

Unity

If so, make me very happy by having the same thoughts,
sharing the same love, and having one mind and purpose.

PHILIPPIANS 2:2 ICB

Kale and his sisters were arguing over which show to watch
on a Saturday morning. Their fighting got so loud it woke
up their parents. When they came downstairs and saw
everyone's frustration, they decided to just turn the TV off.
Kale knew if they had just agreed without arguing, they'd
be sitting with their cereal enjoying their weekend TV time.
Their lack of unity ruined it for everyone.

Unity means being joined together or sharing in the same
purpose or goal. God wants his people to be unified. It
brings him joy when we work together. When we don't have
unity, we might fight or argue over things that don't really
matter. Instead of insisting on your own way, remember
being unified is more important than winning an argument.

How can you work for unity today?

Valued

When you do things, do not let selfishness or pride
be your guide. Instead, be humble and give more honor
to others than to yourselves.

PHILIPPIANS 2:3 NCV

Andre was new at school, and he was nervous about his first
day. When he walked into his first class, he looked around
the room, unsure of where to sit. Another boy raised his
hand, waved him over and told him he could sit in the desk
next to his. When Andre sat down, the boy looked him in
the eye, said hello, and asked him a few questions about his
life. Andre felt noticed and breathed a sigh of relief. Maybe
his first day wouldn't be so bad.

One of the greatest gifts you can give to other people is to
make them feel important. The way you talk to people, the
faces you make, and the things you do all have the power to
make the people around you feel valued. When you listen
to how someone else feels and go out of your way to do
something nice or pay attention to someone who is lonely,
you are treating them the way God would treat them. Today,
instead of focusing only on yourself, try to think of ways to
make someone else feel as if they are the most important
person in the room.

What can you do today to make someone else
feel noticed and valued?

Strong

I pray that from his glorious, unlimited resources he will
empower you with inner strength through his Spirit.

EPHESIANS 3:16 NLT

Raoul and his dad walked through the hospital. They were
visiting some members of their church who were having
some health problems. After leaving the room of one man in
particular, his dad commented on how strong he was. Raoul
felt confused because the man had been tired, sick, and very
weak looking. When he mentioned this to his dad he said,
"His body is sick Raoul, but his spirit is strong because he
trusts in the Lord."

Inner strength is much more important than outer strength.
Anytime your spirit feels weak or tired, you can rely on
God's strength. He will empower you through his Spirit. This
doesn't necessarily mean he will make you physically strong
but he will make you strong on the inside. He will give you
what you need to stay faithful to him and to walk through
difficult things. He will encourage you when you are down
and lift you up when you are overwhelmed.

Have you been relying on your physical strength
or on the strength you get from God?

Creative

The LORD has given them special skills as engravers,
designers, embroiderers in blue, purple, and scarlet thread
on fine linen cloth, and weavers.
They excel as craftsmen and as designers.

EXODUS 35:35 NLT

Alden had two older brothers. One was on the football
team and the other was a straight-A student. They both
had really obvious skills and did a great job at them even
though they were different from each other. Alden felt like
he wasn't really good at anything. He played a few sports but
didn't really care about them, and he struggled to keep up in
school. He spent so much comparing himself to his brothers
he didn't realize what a talented artist he was.

Being creative or artistic is just as important as being strong,
fast, or smart. God gives out all kinds of gifts to his children.
There is not one skill that is more important than another.
Whatever talent you have can be used to glorify God. If you
are unsure what gifts you have been given, ask God to show
you. He loves to teach his children how to honor him with
how they were made. You will be happiest when you are
living in a way that is true to how God made you.

How can you honor God with your gifts today?

Courteous

Let us consider how we can stir up one another to love.
Let us help one another to do good works.

HEBREWS 10:24 NIRV

Guy wanted to be helpful and kind, but he just didn't always notice opportunities to do so. It was a lot easier to focus on himself than to focus on others. When he began to try to pay attention to what other people needed, he started to see opportunities everywhere. His friend was struggling in math class and could use some help. At lunch time, he could sit next to someone who looked lonely. He could teach his younger sister how to be a good friend.

It's not always easy to think of other people. The Bible is full of reminders to help each other because God knows we are likely to only think of ourselves. Paying attention to what other people need takes practice. Being courteous or considerate means you are aware of how you can help the people around you. This can be as simple as opening the door for someone who has full hands or as complex as helping a friend with a serious problem.

What can you do today to practice being courteous?

Loved

The LORD loved your people of long ago very much. You are
their children. And he chose you above all the other nations.
His love and his promise remain with you to this very day.

DEUTERONOMY 10:15 NIRV

Aaron held his knew baby brother in his arms. He'd been
waiting excitedly to meet him, and he was so glad he was
finally here. He loved him already. Within minutes of
meeting him, Aaron knew he would love his brother forever.
If he meant so much to Aaron, he couldn't imagine how God
must feel about him.

You are more loved than you will ever understand. God loves
you fully and perfectly. He knows you inside and out and he
adores you. Nothing can ever change his love for you, and
nothing can ever get in the way of it. If you don't feel God's
love, ask him to show you. He will be faithful to teach you
how much he loves you.

Are you confident in how much God loves you?

Careful

Be very careful how you live.
Do not live like those who are not wise, but live wisely.

EPHESIANS 5:15 NCV

Silas often heard people tell him to make wise choices. When he thought about it, he wasn't really sure what that meant. Wisdom seemed like something he would get as he got older. He figured he was just a kid, and he didn't need to worry about being wise.

No matter your age, you can live carefully in a way that honors God. Making wise decisions isn't something that is just for adults. Ask God to give you wisdom and he will. For you, it might look like learning how to be kind to your siblings or saying no when your friends are doing something they shouldn't. Being wise could look like knowing when to stay quiet or when to speak. These are all things you can practice no matter how old you are. When you ask God for wisdom, he doesn't tell you to wait because you are young. He will always give wisdom to those who ask.

What can you do today to practice being wise?

Compelling

It is Christ's love that fuels our passion and motivates us,
because we are absolutely convinced that he has given his life
for all of us. This means all died with him, so that those who
live should no longer live self-absorbed lives but lives that
are poured out for him—the one who died for us
and now lives again.

2 CORINTHIANS 5:14-15 TPT

Trey really wanted a new bike. He had been saving all of
his money for almost a year. The reward of that shiny,
new bicycle motivated him to keep his money safely in his
bedroom. He'd been tempted to spend it on other things, but
each time the thought of riding his new bike down the road
compelled him to keep saving.

Everything we do is motivated by something. We always
have a reason for the way we act and the choices we make.
Christ's love compels us to live a life that honors him. This
means that his love is what drives us to live a certain way. His
love is the reason we choose to follow him. We are motivated
to love others because of how much Jesus loves us. If you
ever feel unsure about being a Christian, remember the love
of Jesus is the foundation for everything.

Is Christ's love motivating you to live like him
or are you driven by something else?

Discerning

"I, your servant, am here among your chosen people. There are too many of them to count. So I ask that you give me wisdom. Then I can rule the people in the right way. Then I will know the difference between right and wrong. Without wisdom, it is impossible to rule this great people of yours."

1 KINGS 3:8-9 ICB

Ray had a problem. He had been invited to a birthday party this Saturday. He was so excited about it because it was for a new friend, and he was looking forward to getting to spend some more time with him. The issue was that Ray had already promised his sister he would help her with her lemonade stand that very same day. He felt frustrated with his choices and really wanted to do the right thing. When he told his mom about it, she suggested he spend some time asking God for wisdom.

God loves to give wisdom to his children! The Bible is full of examples of people asking God for wisdom and of him helping them make good decisions. You are never expected to figure things out on your own. He wants to help you. When you ask for help, he isn't disappointed that you don't know the answer. He is happy you are depending on him, and he will be faithful to give you wisdom when you ask for it.

Can you ask God for wisdom to help you with a problem you have right now?

Cooperate

Each of us has one body with many parts. And the parts do not all have the same purpose. So also we are many persons. But in Christ we are one body. And each part of the body belongs to all the other parts.

ROMANS 12:4-5 NIRV

Ward's class was working on a group project. His group was really struggling to work together. Everyone was frustrated and annoyed. Their teacher sat down with them to try to help them solve their problem. After talking with them she asked, "Why is Melanie doing the research part when she is more comfortable making the signs? And why is Brandon making signs when he really loves to give presentations?" When they had assigned roles, they hadn't paid attention to each one's skills, which meant that instead of being efficient, they were struggling in roles they didn't like.

When the Bible talks about the body of Christ, it is talking about the worldwide group of believers. Every single person has a unique place. Some people are good at encouraging, while others are good at teaching. Some are gifted to share the Gospel through art, while others share it through their words. Just like assigning tasks with a school group project, we all cooperate together to glorify God and to teach the world about Jesus' love.

How does the body of Christ cooperating glorify God?

AUGUST

Yes, you will suffer for a short time. But after
that, God will make everything right. He will
make you strong. He will support you and
keep you from falling. He is the God who
gives all grace. He called you
to share in his glory in Christ.
That glory will continue forever.

1 PETER 5:10 ICB

Enlightened

I pray that you may understand more clearly. Then you will know the hope God has chosen you to receive. You will know that what God will give his holy people is rich and glorious.

EPHESIANS 1:18 NIRV

A light bulb went off in Omar's mind. He had been struggling through the same math question for the past thirty minutes, and all of a sudden it clicked. He tried to remember how his teacher had explained it, and he looked through his notes from the past week. As he was reading, he realized what the formula meant, and the rest of his homework went smoothly. It felt really good to finally understand something that hadn't made sense before.

In school, you might come across something you don't understand. When that happens, you work toward mastering that skill. You read the problem again, you ask for help, you try another way of solving it. The same problem-solving skills are helpful in your walk with God. When you realize you don't fully grasp the love of God, it is good to spend your time trying to understand it. Read the Word, ask others for help, and pray about understanding what God has done for you. Then you will be enlightened. This means you will grasp more and more truth about God.

As you follow Jesus have you tried to understand him more than you already do?

Flexible

When I am with those who are weak, I share their weakness,
for I want to bring the weak to Christ. Yes, I try to find
common ground with everyone, doing everything
I can to save some.

1 CORINTHIANS 9:22 NLT

Griff was at his best friend's house for a sleepover. As they
were falling asleep, they went around the room telling scary
stories. Partway through the first one, Griff noticed one
of the boys looked really nervous and uncomfortable. He
realized maybe he didn't like the game and so he quickly
suggested they do something different to pass the time. The
boy looked relieved, and the night went on.

One way to be a good friend to those around you is to pay
attention to what other people need. Think about how they
feel and what would make them feel cared for. For example,
if you know your friend is afraid of spiders, maybe when
they come to visit you would leave your pet tarantula in his
cage. Or if you know your brother has a hard time getting his
chores done, you wouldn't brag to him that it only took you
ten minutes to finish yours. Everyone has different strengths
and weaknesses. Being flexible and thinking of others shows
you love them.

When is the last time you were aware of
someone else's weakness?

Favor

A man of kindness attracts favor,
while a cruel man attracts nothing but trouble.

PROVERBS 11:17 TPT

Warren really liked the janitor at his school. He didn't have a fancy job, but Warren had noticed how much he cared for the students. He was always kind, always polite, and he truly seemed to love serving the school. He did his job well, and he never complained. He smiled at everyone who crossed his path, and he was always encouraging the kids that were around him. It was his kindness that made him stand out. Warren knew if this kind janitor ever got another job he would really be missed.

Kindness is attractive. You will always be rewarded for being kind. Other people might notice how you behave and praise you for it, but more importantly God always sees the good things you do. He will have favor on you when you are kind to his children. This means he won't forget, and he will reward you either during your life or when you spend eternity with him.

What is one way you can show kindness to others today?

Blessed

"Blessed are those who trust in the LORD
and have made the LORD their hope and confidence."

JEREMIAH 17:7 NLT

Eduardo was walking out of church when he heard someone tell him to have a blessed day. He wasn't really sure what that meant but he certainly didn't feel very blessed lately. He figured that to consider himself blessed, life would need to be a lot easier than it was. His family didn't have nearly as much other kids seemed to have.

When you hear the word, "blessed," you might think that people are talking about physical things. They might say they are blessed with a good job or a nice house. But being blessed has very little to do with how you feel or what you have. When the Bible talks about being blessed, it is talking about divine favor. This means you are blessed because you are chosen by God to be his child. It has nothing to do with what you have or don't have. You are blessed because of what God has done for you.

Have you been associating blessing with
how much stuff you have or how rich you are?

Riches

Keep your lives free from the love of money, and be satisfied
with what you have. God has said, "I will never leave you;
I will never abandon you."

HEBREWS 13:5 NCV

Cullen had been saving his money for months. He excitedly
went to the store with his mom and picked out a new
skateboard. He was so excited to try it out. He just knew the
skateboard would make him happier than he had ever been.
But before long he wasn't satisfied anymore. He wanted new
shoes for skateboarding and maybe even a cool helmet. Once
again, he started saving his money and thought about how
happy he'd be once he had those things.

You will never be satisfied if you spend your life searching
for riches. You might think buying that next thing you
want will make you happy, but it won't. The happiness that
comes from money is fleeting. This means it does not last.
You might feel good for a short time, but before long you
will need something different to make you happy. Instead
be satisfied with what you have and focus on what God has
given you.

Have you been relying on what you have
to make you happy?

Receive

Everything God created is good.
You shouldn't turn anything down.
Instead, you should thank God for it.

1 TIMOTHY 4:4 NIRV

Kit was really frustrated. He was supposed to go to summer camp but had been unable to because he had gotten sick. Instead of jumping off the dock and making s'mores in the evenings, he was home in bed trying not to cough up a lung. Part way through the week when he still wasn't feeling great, he heard a knock at the door. Before he could get there, his grandma walked in! She surprised him with a visit. If he had gone to camp, he would have missed it.

God loves to give good gifts to his children. Part of receiving gifts from God is realizing you won't always understand a situation like he does. Sometimes, you have to rely on his goodness even if it doesn't make sense to you. Sometimes a situation might seem bad, but actually you just don't see the whole picture. Trust God always and thank him for all he is doing.

What can you do to trust God when
you don't understand or are frustrated?

Loyal

He will kill me. I have no hope.
But I still will defend my ways to his face.

JOB 13:15 ICB

Rocco was invited to play basketball with some of his friends. He was about to go when he saw his neighbor, Landon, sitting outside. They had been friends all of their lives even though they went to different schools and were in different grades. Landon had just lost his grandpa and Rocco knew he was really struggling because they had been very close. Rocco decided to forget about the basketball game and instead he sat with Landon, and they talked about the happy memories he had of his grandpa.

Loyalty means you will be on someone's team no matter what. It means standing with someone even when it would be more comfortable to be somewhere else. One way you can be a loyal friend is by helping others when they are sad. Sometimes people need someone to be with them when they are having a hard time. It would be more fun to go spend time with someone who wants to joke around or play a game but being loyal means you think about what others need and not just what you want.

How can you practice being a loyal friend today?

All

"When you look for me with all your heart,
you will find me."

JEREMIAH 29:13 NIRV

Nikos was supposed to be helping his sister clean the living room, but he quickly became distracted. He had found a Sharpie pen and was doodling something on a sheet of paper while his sister picked up items around him. She asked him to put the pillows back on the couch and he responded with, "Mmhmm, okay, yeah in a minute." He didn't even notice when she put the cushions back herself. She asked him to bring a few cups from the coffee table into the kitchen. He grabbed a cup, walked into the dining room, set it down, and kept drawing. He wasn't focused or devoted to the task which meant he wasn't much help at all.

God doesn't want you to be halfhearted in your search for him. He wants all of your attention and effort. He wants you to know how much you need him and to understand you can't live your life without him. He doesn't want the energy you have left at the end of the day. He doesn't want you to say you'll follow him, only to get distracted when you find something else you'd rather do. Instead, give him your very best, just like he gave his very best to you.

Have you focused all of your attention on God
or are you easily distracted?

Gain

We have small troubles for a while now,
but they are helping us gain an eternal glory
that is much greater than the troubles.

2 CORINTHIANS 4:17 NCV

Bruno loved working with his dad in the garden. It was the time of year when everything was lush, green, and ready to harvest. As they walked through the path with a basket collecting ripe, delicious, veggies, Bruno barely remembered all of the work that had gone into it. In the spring he had been frustrated with the constant watering and weed pulling. Now those troubles seemed so far away as their baskets overflowed.

There might be some days when life feels really difficult. As you get older, you'll probably experience difficulties that you didn't expect. Life isn't always easy, but the Bible promises one day we will trade in all of our troubles, no matter how big or small, for great joy and eternal glory. One day, everything will be made right. Just like the hard work needed for a lush garden, the troubles you face each day are helping you gain something greater. When you feel discouraged, remember Jesus has promised to come back and fix everything.

Have you been focused on the hard work
or the reward that is coming?

Radiant

His teachings make us joyful and radiate his light;
his precepts are so pure! His commands, how they challenge
us to keep close to his heart! The revelation-light of
his word makes my spirit shine radiant.

PSALM 19:8 TPT

Clark watched his little sister open her birthday presents.
She was four today and had been enjoying all of the extra
attention and the special surprises. As she opened a present
from her grandma, he could see her excitement building. She
pulled back the paper and started wide-eyed at a brand-new
doll, just the one she had wanted. His grandma had even
hand made some clothes for it and a blanket to match. For
the rest of the day, his little sister carried her doll around
carefully, her face glowing in happiness. She was full of joy
over the gift she had been given.

In the same way, we should be gloriously happy about what
God has done for us. He is such a good God, and he has
been so generous with his wisdom and kindness. Just like a
child who is radiant because of a good gift she has received,
we should be full of joy over what God has done for us.
If you don't feel that way, ask him to help you. He will be
faithful to show you just how good he is.

Does knowing God make you feel radiant?

Complex

Thank you for making me so wonderfully complex!
Your workmanship is marvelous—how well I know it.

PSALM 139:14 NLT

Sid was struggling to get through math that year. It seemed like no matter how hard he tried he just couldn't wrap his mind around what they were learning. Each time he got back a graded assignment he wasn't happy with, he found himself thinking really negative things about himself. He felt like a failure.

You are wonderfully complex. God created each part of you on purpose. Nothing about you is a mistake. God gave you each of your strengths and weaknesses for a reason. He knows everything about you. He knows exactly who you are and what your life will look like. There is nothing about you he doesn't understand. You are his creation, so don't insult the work he has done. If you ever feel alone or unimportant, remember who your creator is and that he took great care in making you.

How can you thank God today for the way he made you?

Restored

As we wait, we trust in God's royal proclamation to be fulfilled.
There are coming heavens new in quality, and an earth new in
quality, where righteousness will be fully at home.

2 PETER 3:13 TPT

Cosmo watched his mom working on a piece of furniture
she had bought. It was on old dresser with wobbly legs, a
drawer that didn't open the right way, and several chipping
coats of paint. She sanded it down, fixed the broken parts,
and gave it a new coat of paint. When she was done, it
looked as good as. She explained to him this old piece
was worth saving. It was solid, well made, and beautifully
designed. It was good to restore something instead of buying
a new one.

In the same way, one day Jesus will come back, and
everything will be made new. He will restore the entire
earth to the way he intended it to be in the first place. Can
you imagine a perfect earth without any problems? No
more floods or hurricanes. No more pollution, disease, or
extinction. Everything will be completely perfect. He's not
going to make a new earth. He's going to restore all that he's
already made.

What can you do today to look
forward to the day Jesus comes back?

Smart

Go watch the ants, you lazy person.
Watch what they do and be wise.
Ants have no commander.
They have no leader or ruler.
But they store up food in the summer.
They gather their supplies at harvest.

PROVERBS 6:6-8 ICB

Riggs heard adults talk about wisdom a lot. They talked about making wise choices and using wisdom to honor God. When he really thought about it, Riggs would have to admit he thought wisdom was something that would come with age. He figured as he got older, he would become wiser.

The Bible is full of instructions on how to be wise and smart. Just because you are young, doesn't mean you can't be full of wisdom. Wisdom actually has nothing to do with how old you are. There are examples everywhere of how to live in a way that honors God. If you want to be wise, Proverbs is a great place to start. Ask God to give you wisdom and read his Word. Follow the instructions he gives. He hasn't left you alone to figure out your life. He's given you all of the tools you need to live a life that honors him.

How can you increase your wisdom today?

Restraint

If you live without restraint
and are unable to control your temper,
you're as helpless as a city with broken-down defenses,
open to attack.

PROVERBS 25:28 TPT

Ramsay felt like he might explode. His little brother had gone into his room when he wasn't paying attention and had accidentally broken his latest Lego creation. He was so angry about it! He wanted to scream and yell and make sure his brother knew just how angry he was. He could feel his emotions boiling up, ready to spill out at any moment. With all of the self-control he could muster, Ramsay took a deep breath and tried to calm down.

Restraint is the same thing as self-control. It means being able to control your desires. This can be about your emotions or your actions. Just because you want to scream and yell, doesn't mean you should. Just because you want to eat an entire cake, doesn't mean you should. Just because you want to spend all of your money on something silly, doesn't mean you should. When you learn how to control your desires, it will benefit your life. It is good to be to tell yourself "no."

How can you use restraint today?

Still

"Surrender your anxiety.
Be still and realize that I am God.
I am God about all the nations,
and I am exalted throughout the whole earth."

PSALM 46:10 TPT

Burke had a piano recital coming up. In one week he would have to get up in front of a room full of people and play a song he had been working on all year. He was so anxious and overwhelmed about it. All he could think about was how he might mess up, or even completely forget how to play. As he felt himself fill up with worry, he remembered how his dad had taught him to pray about what he was afraid of.

Anxiety is a tricky emotion. It makes you worry and imagine all the ways something could go wrong. Anxiety tells you everything is a mess, and nothing can be fixed. It robs you of your peace and keeps you from trusting God. Don't let anxiety rule your life. Instead, give your worries to God. He is big enough to handle all of them. He can take your worries, and in exchange give you great peace. Let him calm your heart and teach you how to be still.

Is there something you are anxious about
that you can give to God?

More

May God give you more and more grace and peace as you grow in your knowledge of God and Jesus our Lord.

2 PETER 1:2 NLT

Ricki's brother had just gotten home from a birthday party. He couldn't believe it when he saw the goody bag he walked in the door with. "Whoa! You hit the piñata jackpot!" When Ricki asked for some candy, he was shocked when his brother said no. Even though he had so much, he still didn't want to share.

God is not stingy. He is not selfish or cheap. When it comes to his children, he holds nothing back. He could easily keep everything he has for himself but instead he shares it with us. He is always generous with everything he has. He always wants to give you more grace, peace, and wisdom. These are things you can ask him for over and over again. He will never refuse your request. There will never be a point when you ask him for grace or peace, and he just says no. He always wants to give his children more of these things.

Have you ever been nervous to ask for something because you thought the answer would be no?

Vigilant

"Be careful not to spend your time feasting, drinking, or worrying about worldly things. If you do, that day might come on you suddenly, like a trap on all people on earth. So be ready all the time. Pray that you will be strong enough to escape all these things that will happen and that you will be able to stand before the Son of Man."

LUKE 21:34-36 NCV

Jack couldn't wait for his best friend to visit. His family moved to a different state that year and his friend was going to spend one whole week with them over summer break. He would arrive in just a few days. While he waited, Jack excitedly prepared for their time together. He helped blow up an air mattress and made an extra bed in his room. He asked his mom to buy all of their favorite snacks. He made sure he knew where his extra baseball mitt was, and he and his dad even bought tickets to a local game. He did everything he could to prepare for an awesome week with his friend.

To be vigilant means to pay attention and be prepared. Just like you might prepare for a visit from a good friend, you can be vigilant in preparing for Jesus. We are supposed to live in a way that honors him. The Bible says to be ready because we don't know when Jesus will come back.

How can you prepare for Jesus' return today?

Talented

He cared for them with a true heart
and led them with skillful hands.

PSALM 78:72 NLT

Reed was home sick for the third day in a row. His throat
was sore, his body ached, and he had a headache that just
wouldn't go away. He was completely miserable. The only
bright side to being so sick was that he got extra time with
his mom. She watched movies with him, and brought him
bowls of soup. Reed felt loved and well cared for.

If your mom or dad does a good job at taking care of you,
can you imagine how great God is at it? God is not just
competent at being your Father, he is skillful and talented
when it comes to taking care of you. Your parents may be
wonderful, but they aren't perfect. God created you and he
knows you inside and out. He knows exactly what you need
and exactly what all of your days will look like. You can trust
him to provide for you and to help you for all of your life.

When has God shown you that he
takes good care of his children?

Understanding

If you are wise and understand God's ways,
prove it by living an honorable life, doing good works
with the humility that comes from wisdom.

JAMES 3:13 NLT

Chance ran out of storage space in his room and so his mom picked up a bookshelf from the store. It came in a flat box and she asked him to spend part of his afternoon putting it together. He opened the box, tossed the instructions aside, and began screwing boards together in a way that he thought made sense. When he was done, he had an extra board and the whole thing wobbled. Frustrated, he told his mom it was too hard and asked her to do it.

Imagine getting instructions, doing your own thing without looking at them, and then being annoyed when things don't turn out the right way. That might seem obvious, but this is often how we act with the Word of God. He tells us how to be wise and how to live a life that honors him; instead of listening, we still try to do things our own way. Then when things don't work out, we get annoyed and blame God. Instead, we should honor his Word and listen to what he says. This shows you have understanding and wisdom.

Have you ignored God's Word and then been bothered when something doesn't go the right way?

Efficient

Do you see people skilled in their work?
They will work for kings,
not for ordinary people.

PROVERBS 22:29 NCV

Noah was busy cleaning up the equipment after gym class.
He grabbed each ball and put it in the correct bin. He picked
up the flags from football and sorted them by color into the
correct bags. He found a few stray water bottles and carried
them over to the lost and found. Once he was done, his gym
teacher approached him and thanked him for doing such an
efficient job. He said it showed he had good character and he
was thankful for the help.

Someone who is efficient knows how to get a job done
well and on time. An efficient person uses their skills and
accomplishes the task that is in front of them. When you
learn to work in that way, you will find that others notice the
good job you do. Efficiency is one way you can honor God.
Instead of being lazy or careless, do each job with purpose
and make sure you are doing your best. It doesn't matter
whether you are doing your homework, helping your mom
with the dishes, or doing drills at soccer practice, learning to
be efficient is always a good thing.

What's one area of your life where you could
use some efficiency?

Accepted

"The Father gives me the people who are mine. Every one of them will come to me, and I will always accept them."

JOHN 6:37 NCV

No matter what, Paolo knew he could always talk to his dad. No matter what kind of problem he had, his dad was always willing to help. He was ready to listen and do whatever he could to be there for his son. He was gentle and kind when he spoke, and Paolo knew his dad was always on his side. If his dad could be so accepting, he could start to imagine what the kindness of God was really like.

If one person can be so accepting, then imagine what God is like. Anything we are good at, he is even better. When you come to God, he accepts you. He will never turn you away or ask you to leave. He doesn't say to come back when you are a better person or to wait until to you've learned from your mistakes. No matter what, you are always accepted by God.

Do you know that you are accepted by God?

Adapt

When God's people are in need, be ready to help them.
Always be eager to practice hospitality.

ROMANS 12:13 NLT

Cory was the kind of person who always seemed ready to
help. If someone dropped something, he was the first to pick
it up. If someone needed help carrying something, he would
always volunteer. If a classmate forgot their lunch, he would
share his. What made the biggest difference was not that Cory
was really good at helping but that he paid attention to the
people around him. He always noticed when there was a need.

Someone who is adaptable can change how they act
or behave based on what is going on around them. An
adaptable person is always ready for whatever comes their
way. The Bible says we should be adaptable because God says
we should always be ready to help people who are in need.
We should be quick to notice when someone else needs
something. To do this, we need to learn to be focused less on
yourself but to be more aware of the people around you.

How can you practice being adaptable
and ready to help others?

Action

My children, we should love people not only with words and
talk, but by our actions and true caring.

1 JOHN 3:18 NCV

Carter said goodnight to his little brother before turning
off the light. "Goodnight Reid. I love you," he called across
the room. He immediately turned his music on and tried to
fall asleep. When Reid asked him to turn the volume down
he refused. A few minutes later Reid told Carter again that
he couldn't sleep and asked him a second time to turn the
volume down. Carter still said no.

When you say something, your actions should back up your
words. This means if you are going to tell someone you love
them, then you should also show that love in the way you
behave. Thinking about what other people need and want
is one way to show them you love them. If your actions
don't match your words, then what you say doesn't have any
meaning. The same is true about following Jesus. You can't
just say you are a Christian; you also have to change the way
you live so your life shows others that you honor God.

What should you do when your actions
don't line up with your words?

Comfort

All praises belong to the God and Father of our Lord Jesus
Christ. For he is the Father of tender mercy and the God of
endless comfort. He always comes alongside us to comfort
us in every suffering so that we can come alongside those
who are in any painful trial. We can bring them this same
comfort that God has poured out upon us.

2 CORINTHIANS 1:3-4 TPT

Abe's best friend was his dog, Copper. He'd had him since
he was small, and they did everything together. That's why
when Copper passed away, Abe wasn't sure anything would
make him feel better. When his mom sat down to pray with
him he felt a wave of peace. He felt good knowing God was
with him even when he was so sad.

God loves to comfort his children. He promises to be close
to you when you are hurting. He is always by your side,
ready to draw you close and to take care of you. Even when
you feel alone or like no one else cares, God is near. He will
never get tired of you or expect you to be strong on your
own. You can depend on his strength. Then when someone
else goes through something difficult, you can help them by
comforting them in the same way God comforted you.

Have you leaned on the comfort of God lately?

Discipline

Joyful are those you discipline, LORD,
those you teach with your instructions.

PSALM 94:12 NLT

Devin had lost the privilege of playing video games. He'd
gotten into a big fight with his brother and as a result, his
parents had said no to video games for two weeks. He was
really frustrated about it, but he also knew the things he said
to his brother were a big deal. He knew he had messed up. It
was hard to be happy about the discipline he was receiving
but he also knew it did show his parents cared for him.

Even though it might not feel like it at the time, discipline
is good for you. God disciplines you out of love. He knows
what is best for you and he knows how to help you. God's
discipline is not harsh or angry. Even when he is teaching you
something, he is kind and true to his character. This means
he is always merciful, always full of grace, and always loving.

Have you ever thought about how discipline
is good for you?

Cover

Whoever wants to show love forgives a wrong.
But those who talk about it separate close friends.

PROVERBS 17:9 NIRV

Taj sat with his friend Remi at the park. "I'm so mad at Levi," he said. "I still can't believe he ruined my soccer ball." "But you told him it was okay. I thought you'd worked it out," Remi replied. Taj realized even though he hadn't said so to Levi, he was still really angry about the whole thing. Maybe he shouldn't have said everything was fine if it wasn't.

When you have forgiven someone for doing something wrong, it doesn't help to keep talking about. Forgiveness covers others in love and sets them free from their mistake. When an issue has been forgiven and dealt with appropriately, it shouldn't need to keep being brought up again. If you are tempted to keep bringing up an issue, that might mean it hasn't been properly addressed in your heart. Take the time to truly forgive and let God heal your hurts.

Have you forgiven those who have wronged you
or are you carrying hurt around in your heart?

Excellent

He makes grass grow for the cattle
and plants for people to take care of.
That's how they get food from the earth.
There is wine to make people glad.
There is olive oil to make their skin glow.
And there is bread to make them strong.

PSALM 104:14-15 NIRV

Enzo opened his lunch box at school. When he pulled
out his sandwich, he saw a little note from his mom with
a chocolate taped on it. She did little things like that a lot.
Those little gestures made him feel loved and cared for.
He knew she didn't have to do it. It was above and beyond
what was needed. He was thankful for her care and that she
showed him how much she loved in little ways.

God is excellent at taking care of his people. He has filled
the earth with everything we need. Not only that, but he has
given us so many things just to bring us joy. He goes above
and beyond, caring for your needs and giving you things
that will simply make you happy. He didn't have to make
sunsets beautiful, but he did. He didn't have to make our
food delicious, but he did. He isn't just good at loving us; he
is excellent.

Have you thanked God lately for how he
cares for you in such an excellent way?

Responsible

"If you are faithful in little things, you will be faithful in large ones. But if you are dishonest in little things, you won't be honest with greater responsibilities."

LUKE 16:10 NLT

Kade had recently been staying home alone while his mom ran an errand or two. At first, she only left for thirty minutes or an hour. When that went well, she began to let him stay home for longer periods of time. "I know I can trust you," she said. "You've shown me you can make good choices and do the right thing when I'm not here."

If you want to be trusted with big responsibilities, you've got show you can be faithful with smaller ones. This means you need to prove you are capable of doing the right thing in little ways before you are given more to handle. Just like being trusted to stay home alone, there will be many other times in life when you need to prove you are responsible. In those moments, remember the choices you make will impact how much responsibility you are given in the future.

How can you show you are responsible in small ways so you may be trusted in big ways?

Exceptional

"There are many fine women,
but you are better than all of them."

PROVERBS 31:29 NCV

Jerry knew he had an incredible mom. He was thankful for her every day. She was kind, loving, and generous with her time. She made him laugh harder than anyone he knew, and she always knew how to make him smile when he was down. He knew he had an exceptional mom. She made everyone around her feel welcome and loved.

You probably have at least one exceptional woman in your life. Maybe it's your mom, your sister, your grandma, or your aunt. Maybe you have a teacher or a neighbor who is really important to you. No matter what role she plays in your life, she is a gift from God. Take some time today to thank God for the women in your life.

What exceptional women has God put in your life?

Guidance

He shows those who are not proud how to do right.
He teaches them his ways.

PSALM 25:9 ICB

Boaz was in the middle of a tough situation. He had a
disagreement with a friend, and they couldn't seem to figure
it out. He missed his friend and just wanted to go back to
hanging out and having fun. One day after school, Boaz
asked his mom for help. He asked her what to do and was
thankful when she sat down with him, and they prayed
about the situation. He was glad to have someone who was
always willing to help him when he didn't know what to do.

God gives guidance to those who are not proud because they
know they need him. When you are full of pride, you cannot
admit you need help. You are too busy trying to prove you
are the best or you can do it on your own. Needing help isn't
a weakness or a bad thing. Asking for help actually shows
you are wise because you know God is much more capable
than you are. Even when you are strong and talented, God is
still stronger and more talented. No matter your skill level,
lean on him for guidance and he will help you.

In what ways can you trust God for guidance today?

Serenity

May the Lord himself, the Lord of peace, pour into you his
peace in every circumstance and in every possible way.
The Lord's tangible presence be with you all.

2 THESSALONIANS 3:16 TPT

Piers was thankful for the example his parents gave him. He
learned a lot about how to follow Jesus by watching them. He
noticed that even when life was difficult, they chose to trust
God. As a result, they were very peaceful people. He noticed
that when problems came up, the first thing they did was ask
God for help. They knew no matter what, God was there to
help them. That was the kind of person that Piers wanted to be.

Following Jesus doesn't mean you will magically always have
the right answers or you will always know what to do. It does
mean that no matter what you can have peace. He promises
that in every circumstance, you can trust him and he will be
near to you. You can have serenity because you know God is
in control, and he loves you.

Have you experienced the peace
that comes from trusting God?

SEPTEMBER

My mind and my body
may become weak.
But God is my strength.
He is mine forever.

PSALM 73:26 ICB

Citizen

You Gentiles are no longer strangers and foreigners.
You are citizens along with all of God's holy people.
You are members of God's family.

EPHESIANS 2:19 NLT

A few years ago, Luke's aunt married a man from Canada.
Luke loved learning about what life was like in another
country. He liked listening to his new uncle's stories about
his favorite foods, places, and traditions. Even though his
uncle had moved the US after they got married, he was still
really proud to be a Canadian citizen.

A lot of people are proud of the country they are from. They
like to talk about it and explain why it's the best in some
ways. They are a proud citizen. It's good to love the place
you are from but it's more important to realize that your
citizenship is actually in heaven. No matter what country
you call home, the most important place you belong to is the
family of God. Your home on earth is temporary but your
home in heaven is where you will live forever.

Are you a proud citizen of heaven?

Relax

That's where he restores and revives my life.
He opens before me the right path
and leads me along in his footsteps of righteousness
so that I can bring honor to his name.

PSALM 23:3 TPT

School would be starting next week and Niko had been thinking about how great the summer had been. He had gone fishing with his dad, he had watched cartoons in the mornings, and he'd even taken a couple naps in the hammock in their backyard. He had relaxed with the best of them. The last school year had been extra hard and so it had felt really good to have some downtime. Now that he was back at school, he felt ready to do his best and to learn what he needed to learn.

God doesn't expect you to work hard for every moment of your life. He created you to need rest. Rest is a good gift from God. It does not make you lazy and it does not mean you aren't productive or hardworking. The truth is if you want to honor God then you need to learn how to rest. This can mean many different things. Maybe you take a nap, relax with a book, or watch a movie. Maybe you take a walk or spend some quiet time outside. Rest can come in many shapes and forms.

Did you know that rest can honor God?

Success

Their purpose is to teach people to live
disciplined and successful lives,
to help them do what is right, just, and fair.

PROVERBS 1:3 NLT

Terry wanted to be just like his dad when he grew up.
Everyone loved his dad. He had noticed that when his dad
walked into a room, people smiled and looked happy. He
had a pretty normal job, and they didn't have a lot of money,
but Terry's dad was wildly successful. He was kind, honest,
and made other people feel loved and important.

When you think of success, what comes to mind? Do you
imagine someone with a lot of money or power? Does a
successful person have their dream job or a huge house?
The way we think about success isn't always how God thinks
about it. He says that someone is successful when they
do what is right, just, and fair. This means we should be
thinking more about if our actions please God than if they
make us money. To honor God, we should be doing our best
to do the right thing and to treat others well.

Do you see kindness, honesty, and tenderness
as the best measurement of success?

Reasonable

The wisdom that comes from God is first of all pure, then peaceful, gentle, and easy to please. This wisdom is always ready to help those who are troubled and to do good for others. It is always fair and honest.

JAMES 3:17 NCV

Madden had a problem he didn't know how to solve. He needed to decide which sport he wanted to play during the school year. His parents had said he could only pick one and he didn't know what to do. He'd been thinking about it for days and he still felt stuck. He had asked a few people, but their opinions didn't help him. When he finally remembered to ask God for wisdom, he wondered why he hadn't done that earlier.

God is always ready to help you. No problem is too big or too small for him. His wisdom is reasonable, perfect, and always available to you. You can ask him for wisdom whenever you want. He always knows what to do and how to help. Sometimes asking him for wisdom is the last thing we think of when we have a problem. It sounds simple, but it's easy to forget that he should be our very first thought in times of indecision and trouble. It takes practice to remember to go to him first.

When is the last time you asked God for help?

Try

Try your best to be found pure and without blame.
Be at peace with God.

2 PETER 3:14 NIRV

Reece was very aware of his mistakes. There was so much he wanted to do perfectly but no matter how hard he tried, he still seemed to fall short. He felt like he should be doing better in school, and he was tired of messing up. After a frustrating day he talked to his mom about how he felt. She was surprised by how upset he was. She hugged him and explained how proud they were of him for his hard work. She said that the effort he put into school was just as important as the grade at the end of the year.

The Bible says to try to live without blame. It's important to notice that God doesn't say, "Be perfect or else." Sometimes when we think about how to please God we start to see him as a ruler or just someone with a lot of power. You might think you have to be perfect or God won't be happy with you. The truth is he simply asks you to try. He's just like a loving mom who is proud of you all of the time. He knows your limits and he knows each mistake you will make for the rest of your life. He loves you and accepts you, not because of what you can do, but because you are his child.

Did you know God is not ashamed of you
or your mistakes?

Virtue

"He did no sin.
He never lied."
1 PETER 2:22 ICB

Phillip studied for his math test, but after a short time he got distracted and decided to play basketball instead. When he sat down to take the test, he really struggled through it. He made a lot of mistakes, and he knew he should have stayed focused during his study session. When he handed his test in his teacher told him he would be getting a perfect grade because another boy in the class had worked really hard and had gotten everything right. Phillip was shocked!

Can you imagine that scenario? In a similar way, we get to benefit from what Jesus has done for us even though we didn't do any of the work. Having virtue means doing the right thing and behaving wisely. Jesus has more virtue than any of us ever will have. He never sinned and he never lied. Can you imagine complete perfection? Jesus always did the right thing. He never made any mistakes and everything he did honored God perfectly. Because of his perfection, your sins are forgiven. His great sacrifice is why you get to be close to God.

Did you know Jesus' perfection is now your perfection?

Worth

Recognize the value of every person and continually show love to every believer. Live your lives with great reverence and in holy awe of God. Honor your rulers.

1 PETER 2:17 TPT

Fritz was well liked at school. It wasn't because he was super smart or the captain of the football team. He wasn't the funniest person in the room or the most talented artist. Fritz was well liked because he was the kind of person who treated everyone the same. No matter what, he was friendly, kind, and helpful. He made every person he talked to feel important and special.

Every single person you meet has great value. You don't get to decide the worth of others. God is the only one who gets to decide that. Your job is not to choose whether or not someone deserves your love. God says we are supposed to continually show love to every person. It can be tempting to change how you treat people depending on how you feel about them or whether or not you like them. Doing that doesn't show God's love to others. Instead, honor God by treating everyone as though they have unlimited worth.

How can you show the people around you they are important to God?

Stunning

In your glory and grandeur go forth in victory!
Through your faithfulness and meekness
the cause of truth and justice will stand.
Awe-inspiring miracles are accomplished by your power,
leaving everyone dazed and astonished!

PSALM 45:4 TPT

Tucker kept hearing that God was always working. His pastor would talk about it, his parents would talk about it, and his youth leader would talk about it. He believed what they were saying but he just didn't really understand it. Life seemed pretty normal, and he hadn't witnessed any miracles lately. What could God be doing?

God does glorious and stunning things all of the time. If you pay attention you will start to see he is always working. He is healing the sick, he is comforting the hurting, and he is changing hearts all over the world. God does big miracles, but he is also the one behind the small miracles in everyday life. He makes the sun rise and set, he sends rain for plants to grow, and he gives you the breath in your lungs. If you feel like God isn't doing anything, ask him to show you. He will be faithful to open your eyes to his good works.

What is something God has done for you today?

Reputation

Never let loyalty and kindness leave you!
Write them deep within your heart.
Then you will find favor with both God and people,
and you will earn a good reputation.

PROVERBS 3:3-4 NLT

Nathan was nervous about going to high school. He knew he
would do fine in all of his classes, and he was excited about
trying out for different sports. What made him nervous were
the things he heard about some of the older kids. A few of
them had reputations for being unkind and even cruel to the
newcomers. He hadn't even met them before and yet he'd
been hearing about their behavior for months.

Your reputation is who other people believe you are. You
can have a good reputation or a bad reputation. You can be
known as someone who is kind, loyal, generous, and helpful.
Or you can be known as someone who complains and is
selfish, rude, and unkind. The way you behave and treat
people matters. When you strive to have a good reputation,
you will honor God.

What kind of reputation do you have?

Remember

Be careful! Watch out and don't forget the things you have
seen. Don't forget them as long as you live, but teach them to
your children and grandchildren.

DEUTERONOMY 4:9 NCV

Theo was so angry with his sister. Lately they'd been fighting
non-stop and just couldn't seem to get along. He stormed
into his room after one of their arguments and plopped
down on his bed in a huff. As he sat there fuming, something
across the room caught his attention. It was a painting on his
wall that his sister had done for him. It was of Theo and his
dog. Theo loved his dog! Looking at the painting made Theo
remember that his sister did care for him. He felt encouraged
and went out to try to talk to her about it.

Remember an act of kindness can help when you are
frustrated with someone. In the same way, when you find
yourself discouraged about your relationship with God, it's
probably because you've forgotten all of the wonderful things
he has done. We are really good at forgetting good things
and focusing on what is hard or frustrating. Instead, take the
time to remember who God is and what he has done. Write
those things down so when you are having a bad day you can
look back and see how faithful God has been.

Have you spoken to anyone lately about
the good things God has done for you?

Resilient

When troubles of any kind come your way, consider it an
opportunity for great joy. For you know that when your faith
is tested, your endurance has a chance to grow.

JAMES 1:2-3 NLT

Foster wanted to quit running. He was tired and his legs
hurt. He signed up for the track team because his best friend
was doing it and he hadn't realized how hard it would be.
He finished his practice and crawled into bed that night
with sore muscles. Two days later, he was shocked when it
actually seemed easier to run than it had at the last practice.
He'd gotten stronger! He was encouraged by his progress and
decided to keep going.

Being resilient means you don't give up when things get
difficult. It means refusing to quit even when you want to.
Your life won't always be easy and there will be times when
a situation is really discouraging. When something difficult
happens, it is tempting to focus only on the ways that the
situation is bad or hard. Instead, focus on how you can learn
and grow. Then the next time something hard happens you
will be even stronger.

What helps you keep going when you want to quit?

Sincere

Unlike many people, we aren't selling God's word to make money. In fact, it is just the opposite. Because of Christ we speak honestly before God. We speak like people God has sent.

2 CORINTHIANS 2:17 NIRV

Apollo sat in church next to his parents. The pastor was talking about all Jesus had done for them. Apollo realized he spent most of his prayer time talking to God about all the things he wanted. He had high hopes for what God would do for him, but he hadn't put much thought into what had already been done.

We don't follow Jesus because of what we get from him. We follow Jesus because of what he has already done for us. God is not a genie who is there just to give you what you want. A sincere faith knows that God has already given you the greatest gift you could ever ask for—salvation through Jesus. If you find yourself mostly asking God for things, try thanking him for something he has already done for you. Spend some time thinking about who he is and praise him for his character.

How can you focus less on what you want and more on what has been done for you already?

Divine

Ever since the world was created, people have seen the earth
and sky. Through everything God made, they can clearly see
his invisible qualities—his eternal power and divine nature.
So they have no excuse for not knowing God.

ROMANS 1:20 NLT

Crispin loved being outside. In all kinds of weather, he would
rather be outside than inside. He wanted to have his toes in
the grass and be looking for his next adventure. He loved
summer vacation because it meant from sunrise to sunset, he
could be playing, or hiking, or swimming with his siblings.
He was so thankful God had made creation so wonderful.

The Bible says we can know who God is by looking at all that
he has made. His creation, the earth, and every living thing
on it, tells us about who he is. Creation shows us he is wise,
powerful, kind, and beautiful. We can understand a little
bit of the divine by simply looking around us and paying
attention to all he has made. If you ever feel discouraged in
your relationship with God, take some time to appreciate
his creation.

Have you taken time to appreciate creation lately?

Driven

Without faith living within us it would be impossible to please
God. For we come to God in faith knowing that he is real and
that he rewards the faith of those who passionately seek him.

HEBREWS 11:6 TPT

AJ wanted to go to summer camp next year. He had never
been and his mom promised that if he kept his grades up
this year, he would get to go. School had just started, and he
was determined to reach his goal. The thought of spending
a whole week fishing and hiking with his friends motivated
him to do a good job at school. He was driven by his goal of
getting to go away for an entire week.

Everybody has something that drives them. This means people
are motivated by different things. Some people might be
motivated by making money. Others might be driven by the
desire to have a successful career. You might be driven by the
desire to go to camp, or to be on the football team, or to one
day have your driver's license. As a Christian, let your faith in
God motivate everything you do. When your life is defined
by who you believe God is, then you will notice that what's
important to him will also be important to you. When your
faith is what motivates you, everything else will fall into place.

What drives you? What is your motivation?

Ethical

"Well, then," Jesus said, "give to Caesar what belongs
to Caesar, and give to God what belongs to God."
His reply completely amazed them.

MARK 12:17 NLT

Laurent had noticed everyone was talking about the election
lately. There was a lot he didn't understand but he could tell
everyone seemed to have a strong opinion. When he asked
his parents what they thought, they said that no matter who
won, God would still be the true ruler. They explained that
as members of God's family, they were called to respect their
leaders even if the person they voted for didn't win.

God is your true King and he is the one whom we are
supposed to serve above all. This doesn't mean you can
ignore the leadership of the people. We are told to "give
to Caesar what belongs to Caesar." This means you should
follow the laws of the land and respect those in authority. It
is ethical to follow laws. This means it is the right choice to
listen to the rules that are in place.

How can you honor God when you're thinking or talking
about the leadership in your community or country?

Conscientious

Don't fail to use the gift the Holy Spirit gave you…
Keep on doing these things.
Give them your complete attention.
Then everyone will see how you are coming along.

1 TIMOTHY 4:14-15 NIRV

Zane had spent all summer focused on soccer. He had lived and breathed the sport. He'd spent hours each day perfecting his skills and trying to get better. He had high hopes for this year's soccer team, and he wanted to play his part well. When he came across something he didn't do well, he tried harder. He didn't give up because he wanted to make sure he did his very best to help his team win. Zane was a conscientious team member.

Someone who is conscientious wants to do what is right. A conscientious person is thorough and pays attention to detail. God asks you to be conscientious when it comes to the gifts he has given you. He wants you to pay attention to how he has made you and the strengths he has given you. Just like you might perfect your skills in a sport, you can perfect the gifts God has given you. You can use your gifts to honor him and to serve him well. Today, think about what gifts he has given you and how you can hone them as you grow.

What is something God has given you specifically?

Surrounded

The LORD your God has blessed everything you have done;
he has protected you while you traveled through this great
desert. The LORD your God has been with you for the past
forty years, and you have had everything you needed.

DEUTERONOMY 2:7 NCV

Lars sat by the campfire with his family. It was nearly fall and
the days were slowly getting chillier. The evening air felt cold,
but the warmth of the fire wrapped around him. It didn't
matter how cold it was, he felt safe and cozy in the light of
the fire. Lars thought about how God's love was a lot like that
warmth; it surrounded him on all sides and brought warmth
and light to his life.

You are never alone. Even if you feel lost or hopeless, God
is with you. He surrounds you and protects you. He is
always with you and is always mindful of you. This means
he is always thinking about you. He never forgets you or is
too busy to pay attention to you. Isn't that incredible? The
Creator of the entire universe is thinking about you. When
you are down or are having a bad day, remember you are
surrounded by the love of a great God.

Do you feel surrounded by God's love today?

Certain

We are convinced that every detail of our lives is continually woven together for good, for we are his lovers who have been called to fulfill his designed purpose.

ROMANS 8:28 TPT

Timo grabbed a jacket from the hook by the door. He stuffed it in his backpack and went to school. When he got there, his brother found him in the hallway. "Hey, you have my grey jacket. Can I have it back?" Timo insisted he had grabbed his own black jacket and tried to explain it to his brother. His brother didn't believe him, but he was certain he had the right one. He unzipped his backpack and there it was, the black jacket. His brother left frustrated but Timo knew he had been right all along.

When you are certain of something, you will have a lot of confidence in it. No matter who tries to tell you differently, you won't change your mind. This is how you should look at the way God is and what he has done for you. You can be certain he is good and as his son, you are called to live a life which honors him. He is concerned about every detail in your life, and he is always working for you. When you are certain of this, your faith will be full of confidence, and you won't be shaken when storms come your way.

What is a characteristic of God
that you are certain about?

Cherished

He takes care of his flock like a shepherd.
He gathers the lambs in his arms.
He carries them close to his heart.
He gently leads those that have little ones.

ISAIAH 40:11 NIRV

Gunnar loved visiting his grandparent's farm. Over the years, his grandpa had been teaching him how to care for the different animals they owned. His grandfather was a big, burly man but he was gentle and kind in his ways. He paid attention to each animal's needs, and he expertly made sure they were happy and healthy. His care made Gunnar think about how much God cares for each of his children.

God is a good Father. He is like a shepherd who takes care of his flock. He's pays attention to what they need, and he keeps them safe. He values each of his children including you and will never give up on any of them. He cherishes you and promises to lead you all the days of your life. He will never leave you, but he will carry you close to his heart.

How has God shown you he cares for you?

Accountability

Confess your sins to each other and pray for each other so that you may be healed. The earnest prayer of a righteous person has great power and produces wonderful results.

JAMES 5:16 NLT

Ace hated to admit when he was wrong. The idea of getting into to trouble made him so nervous he sometimes would just lie or stretch the truth. He would try to make it sound like it didn't really matter whenever he had done something wrong. Lately his parents had been talking to him about accountability. He was slowly learning how to honest about his mistakes even though it was hard.

Accountability means being responsible for your actions. When you are accountable for your sins, you are open and honest about what you have done wrong. You own up to your mistakes and you don't try to make it seem like it wasn't a big deal. The Bible tells us to be accountable to each other. That means we are supposed to talk to each other about the things we've done wrong. Be honest about your mistakes and pray for each other and then you will find freedom from those mistakes.

Who can you talk to you about the things you've done wrong?

Ask

"Ask, and God will give to you. Search, and you will find.
Knock, and the door will open for you."

MATTHEW 7:7 NCV

Beck felt worried about his guitar recital. He'd been practicing
and he felt like he knew his song really well, but the idea of
playing it in front of so many people made him nervous. As
he was preparing for it the day before, he remembered he
could ask God for help. He prayed God would help him to
stay calm and would take his worries away. When he asked
for help, he felt a wave of peace. He knew God is bigger than
he is and would take care of all his worries.

Learn how to ask God for what you need. Develop the habit
of going to him first. When you ask him for something,
it is like you are putting it in his hands. This means you
don't have to worry about it anymore. He is big enough to
handle whatever you need. It's easy to forget he is right there,
waiting for you to come to him.

When you are worried, how can you remember
to ask God for what you need?

Respect

Lord, teach me what you want me to do.
And I will live by your truth.
Teach me to respect you completely.

PSALM 86:11 ICB

Tai sat in an assembly at school. They were there to listen to a guest speaker. Tai couldn't remember who it was, and he didn't really feel like listening. For the first few minutes he chatted with his friends and didn't really pay attention. A teacher caught his eye and the look on his face told Tai he should probably be quiet. As he began to listen to the speaker's story, he realized he deserved Tai's admiration and respect. He sat quietly for the rest of the assembly and listened to what was being shared with him.

The more you get to know God, the more you'll realize how worthy he is. He deserves all of your praise and worship. He has done great and wonderful things and he deserves all of the respect we can give him. You can't respect someone if you don't understand who they are or what they've done. Respect comes from knowing the truth about someone. As you grow older and get to know God more, respect will become easier and easier.

What can you do today to
get to know God in a better way?

Alive

"Just as the Father raises the dead and gives them life,
so also the Son gives life to those he wants to."

JOHN 5:21 NCV

Malik said something unkind to his sister. After they
talked about it and he apologized, he also asked God for
forgiveness. He knew God could wipe away his sins. He
thought about all of the things he had done wrong even
just that week. He'd fought with his sister, refused to clean
his room when asked, and lied about having his homework
done. It wasn't hard to come up with a list of mistakes. He
was so thankful he could be free from his sins, big and small,
and he didn't need to keep track of them of them all.

You were once dead in your sin but now you are alive because
of Jesus. This means that without Jesus' sacrifice, you would
have been responsible for every single thing you've ever done
wrong. Because of what Jesus has done for you, you have
been forgiven of your sins. You have been set free from your
wrongs. You are free, alive, and able to be close to God.

Have your thanked God lately
for the life you have in Christ?

Filled

I pray that the God who gives hope will fill you
with much joy and peace while you trust in him.

ROMANS 15:13 NCV

Today was Aurelio's birthday and he was anxiously sitting
at the table, watching his mom carry a big chocolate cake
across the room. It had a flickering candle on top and his
whole family was singing the happy birthday song. After he
blew out the candle, his mom began to cut the cake. She cut
off the tiniest sliver and gave it Aurelio. She chuckled as she
saw the look on his face, winked at him, and cut him a bigger
piece. It made him laugh. Of course, she wouldn't give him
the world's smallest bite of cake on his birthday when there
was an entire delicious cake right in front of him.

God doesn't want to give you a little taste of joy. He doesn't
want you to sort of know what peace is. He wants to fill you
with joy and peace. He doesn't want to give you just a small
portion of what he has. He wants you to be overflowing with
good things. He is a kind and generous Father who wants
only the best for his children. He is not a harsh ruler who is
waiting for you to mess up. He is full of joy and peace and he
wants the same for you.

Have you been expecting small things from God
when he wants to do big things in your life?

Acknowledged

"What if someone says in front of others that they know me?
I will also say in front of my Father who is in heaven
that I know them."

MATTHEW 10:32 NIRV

Cree was talking with a friend at recess. His friend was telling him about his weekend. He said he went to the local bike shop and bought a new bike. He told a story about the owner of the shop and how kind he was. He taught him how to fill the tires and to do some basic repairs on the bike. Cree smiled, "Yeah, that's my grandpa. He's the best." Cree was proud of his grandpa and was happy to admit that he knew him.

To acknowledge someone means to recognize or admit to who they are. It means if someone says, "Jesus is not the son of God," you would tell them the truth. When you acknowledge Jesus, he will acknowledge you. You can tell other people about knowing Jesus just like you might tell them you know a friend or a relative. Knowing in your heart that he is the Son of God and telling others about who he is shows you have put your faith in him. It can sometimes take courage to talk about your faith, but you don't have to be afraid; God is on your side.

When the time comes, are you
proud to acknowledge Jesus?

Confirmed

This is no empty hope, for God himself is the one
who has prepared us for this wonderful destiny.
And to confirm this promise, he has given us the Holy Spirit,
like an engagement ring, as a guarantee.

2 CORINTHIANS 5:5 TPT

Lester trusted when his grandma made him a promise.
She said on his birthday they would go get milkshakes. He
believed what she said and knew it would happen. She had
always kept her word and he knew she was trustworthy.
Lester knew if he could put his trust in his grandma, then he
could trust God's promises even more.

The Bible is full of promises God has made. You might wonder
how we are so sure God will keep his promises. One of the
ways we know God is trustworthy is that he has given us the
Holy Spirit. The Holy Spirit was given to us to teach, guide,
and point us to truth. God confirmed his promise that Jesus
would come back again by leaving us with the Holy Spirit.

Did you know the Holy Spirit is confirmation
that God keeps his promises?

Witness

You have heard me teach things that have been confirmed by many reliable witnesses. Now teach these truths to other trustworthy people who will be able to pass them on to others.

2 TIMOTHY 2:2 NLT

Chen saw the craziest thing happen. While he was walking home from school, he saw a man riding a unicycle down the sidewalk. While he rode, he played the guitar and was singing a song. When he got home, he told his sister about it and she said, "Yeah, right. I don't believe you." She changed her mind when later that evening, their neighbor shared the same story.

When more than one person sees something happen, it makes the story more believable. If only one person saw it, it's easy to question whether or not it actually happened. When others can confirm the details, we tend to believe it's true. The accounts in the Bible are told from many different people. Part of why you can trust the Word of God is that the events were witnessed and confirmed by a lot of people.

What's another way you know
the Word of God is trustworthy?

Encourage

When we get together, I want to encourage you in your faith,
but I also want to be encouraged by yours.

ROMANS 1:12 NLT

Alfonso was thankful for the youth group he went to. Each
week he knew as soon as he walked in the room he would be
loved and encouraged. It was a place that felt like home. His
closest friends were there, and he loved knowing that by the
end of the night he would feel lifted up and strengthened.
They shared how their week was going, they prayed for each
other, and they learned more about who Jesus is.

We need each other. God made us to live in community with
other believers. You aren't supposed to live life on your own.
You aren't supposed to have all of the answers or to be able
to figure things out alone. You need to be encouraged by
other people who are following Jesus. In the same way, other
people need to be encouraged by you. You can encourage
others by lifting them up, saying something kind, and
reminding them of what God thinks about them.

Do you have someone, or a group of people, in your
life who encourage you in your faith?

Active

God's word is alive and working and is sharper than a double-edged sword. It cuts all the way into us, where the soul and the spirit are joined, to the center of our joints and bones. And it judges the thoughts and feelings in our hearts.

HEBREWS 4:12 NCV

Bobby found the Bible to be kind of boring. He hadn't read much of it because he found it difficult to stay focused. When he shared this with his dad, he prayed with Bobby that the Word would come alive to him and that he would be encouraged by the truth. He reminded him that every part of the Bible is good for teaching, and that reading it doesn't have to be a chore or an item we cross off of a list.

The Bible is not just a bunch of words on a page. It's not just a collection of stories about people who lived a long time ago. God's Word is alive. It can speak to your heart and judge your thoughts and feelings. Reading God's Word fills your mind with truth and allows you to make decisions that honor him. When you are familiar with what God has said, you will be confident in his love and well equipped to face any troubles that may come your way.

If you're struggling to read the Word, how can you change your perspective?

Cheerful

Let the message about Christ live among you like a rich treasure. Teach and correct one another wisely. Teach one another by singing psalms and hymns and songs from the Spirit. Sing to God with thanks in your hearts.

COLOSSIANS 3:16 NIRV

Alistair adored his older brother. He was his favorite person in the entire world. He loved everything about him. Most of all, he loved how he made him feel special and important. He always had time to hang out with him and he never made him feel like he didn't want him around. Just thinking about spending time with his brother made Alistair smile.

Just like knowing certain people fill you with joy, Jesus wants his relationship with you to cause you to be cheerful. Following Jesus is not supposed to be heavy, boring, or a burden. Instead, God wants you to be full of joy. He wants the gospel to be like a treasure in your life. He wants you to be cheerful about your relationship with him. The Gospel is serious, but it is also the happiest news you will ever hear. It is full of life, joy, and goodness. Knowing who Jesus is should make your heart feel cheerful. Today, take some time to thank God for the good news of the gospel.

Does knowing God make you cheerful?

OCTOBER

I can do all this
by the power of Christ.
He gives me strength.

PHILIPPIANS 4:13 NIRV

Sharpen

As iron sharpens iron,
so people can improve each other.

PROVERBS 27:17 NCV

Boris was not very good at memorizing. For Sunday school, they had been working on learning a passage from Romans and he was really struggling. Normally, he would be really frustrated about how difficult it was for him, but then he remembered his best friend Van was actually really good at memorizing. He asked him if they could work on it and together they learned the passage in one afternoon. He was thankful for a friend who was willing to help.

We are supposed to make each other better. We are all uniquely made, with individual talents and gifts. God is glorified when we use those gifts to encourage each other and to help each other live in a way that pleases God. You can do this by comforting someone who is hurting, encouraging someone who is down, or teaching someone who needs help. Our gifts are not meant to be boasted about or flaunted. Instead, as members of the same team, we lift each other up and do our best to get better together.

How can you use your gifts to sharpen other believers?

Forgiveness

Higher than the highest heavens— that's how high your tender
mercy extends! Greater than the grandeur of heaven above is
the greatness of your loyal love, towering over all who fear you
and bow down before you! Farther than from a sunrise to a
sunset— that's how far you've removed our guilt from us.

PSALM 103:11-12 TPT

Earlier in the year Brennan had gotten into an argument
with his best friend. They had both said some things that
were unkind. Eventually they apologized to each other and
moved on but Brennan couldn't seem to let it go. This made
him feel even more thankful to God for the miraculous
way he wipes our sins away. He asked God to help him be
gracious and forgiving towards his friend.

As a follower of Jesus, you have been forgiven of your sins.
God has wiped them away. They are completely gone. Not
only does he forgive your sins, but he can remove guilt. That
means that once you've asked God for forgiveness you don't
need to carry around the burden of what you've done wrong.
You can put it in his hands and be free. He won't hold it
against you or bring it back up.

How can you practice forgiveness
in the way God models it?

Tolerant

Don't you see how wonderfully kind, tolerant, and patient God is with you? Does this mean nothing to you? Can't you see that his kindness is intended to turn you from your sin?

ROMANS 2:4 NLT

Sven knew his parents trusted him. He was the oldest kid in his family and so he had more responsibility than his younger siblings. He also got to enjoy some perks that they didn't get yet. He was allowed to stay home alone, and to go to bed later than everyone else. Just because his parents let him do these things didn't mean he could do whatever he wanted. He wanted to keep his privileges and so he respected their rules. He knew if he took advantage of the freedom he had, it probably wouldn't last long.

We all fall short of God's perfection. We make mistakes each day and often fail to live up to his standards. Even with all of our troubles God is patient and kind. He knows exactly how many mistakes you will make, and he is gentle with you. He is not angry or harsh. He is always ready to forgive you when you ask. This doesn't mean you can do whatever you want just because you know God will forgive you. God's kindness should motivate you to do the right thing.

Does God's tolerance and kindness motivate you to turn from your sin?

Innocent

Be wise as to what is good and innocent
as to what is evil.

ROMANS 16:19 NLT

Ivan sat around the campfire with his family. The cold fall air was making him shiver so he pushed his chair a little closer to the warmth of the flames. As the evening got later and later, he got colder and colder. Every few minutes, he moved his chair closer. "You're going to burn yourself if you go any closer," his mom warned. Ivan didn't care, he was freezing. He shoved his chair within a few inches of the edge of the fire and sure enough, a spark shot out and landed on his leg. He wished he'd listened to the warning from his mom.

Sometimes it is tempting to inch as close as possible to the fire and hope you don't get burned. The same can be true about sin. We often try to get as close as we can to sin and hope we don't go too far. Being innocent to what is evil is not always easy to do. The world is full of opportunities to do the wrong thing. It's not hard to find ways to sin. Being innocent to evil means you stay as far away from what is wrong as possible. God knows this is what's best for you.

Have you ever tried to get as close to sin as possible,
hoping you get away with it?

Insightful

Help each other with your troubles.
When you do this, you truly obey the law of Christ.

GALATIANS 6:2 ICB

"God, help me to see opportunities to show others about your love," Brock prayed in the morning before he went to school. He wanted to be the kind of person who noticed when someone needed help. That day he saw all kinds of ways he could encourage others. He helped a boy in math class with a difficult problem. He complimented his friend's basketball skills. He picked up the books of someone who was carrying too much and had dropped everything. He realized when he paid attention there were endless ways to help others.

We are designed to need each other. You cannot manage life on your own. You need the love and support of the people around you. In the same way, you are meant to help others. You have what it takes to make other people's lives better. Ask God and he will give you insight into how you can help the people around you. Maybe someone needs an encouraging word, a helping hand, or even just a friendly face.

Have you been insightful towards the troubles of others?

Approval

As soon as Jesus was baptized, he came up out of the water.
Then heaven opened, and he saw God's Spirit coming down
on him like a dove. And a voice from heaven said, "This is
my Son, whom I love, and I am very pleased with him."

MATTHEW 3:16-17 NCV

Crew had worked all month on his science project. It had
turned out exactly as he had wanted, and he was so excited to
present it to his class. Their parents were invited to watch the
presentations and when he looked out into the crowd, he saw
his dad's smiling face. When he finished his presentation, his
dad gave him a high five and he knew he was proud of him.
He knew his dad approved of his hard work.

God approved of Jesus. This means he was proud of what
he had done and who he was. He looked at him and said,
"Good job!" God also gives you his approval because of what
Jesus has done for you. Jesus died on the cross so you could
have the approval of God. His sacrifice means God looks
at you and says, "Good job! I am proud of you. You are my
son." Without Jesus, we cannot have God's approval. Today,
take some time to thank God for what he has done for you.

Do you feel God's pride and approval over you?

Justice

Your goodness is as high as the mountains.
Your justice is as deep as the great ocean.
LORD, you protect both people and animals.

PSALM 36:6 NCV

Martin was watching the news with his family. It seemed like every other segment was about something horrible happening in the world. He didn't understand how so many bad things could be going on at once. It was both stressful and really sad. When they finally turned the TV off, Martin's dad said they should take a moment to pray. They asked God to be near to the brokenhearted and to bring justice to all of the wrongs that had been done.

Justice is doing what is right and fair. God is always just. He always does what is right and fair. The world is full of injustice. If you look around for even a little bit you will see plenty of examples of bad things happening. This can be discouraging and frustrating. Remember God has not forgotten anything. We can trust him and let him handle the wrongs of others. He is just and will take care of his people.

Have you ever been discouraged by
something bad happening in the world?
How can you trust the justice of God?

Hardworking

The plans of people who work hard succeed.
You can be just as sure that those in a hurry
will become poor.

PROVERBS 21:5 NIRV

Joaquin was mowing the lawn for his dad. It had been a long day and he didn't feel like doing it anymore. He figured his dad wouldn't notice if he cut a few corners and avoided a few of the spots at the back of their property. When he was putting the lawnmower away his dad asked how it went. He felt guilty for not doing his best and told his dad what had happened. His dad explained that even though he was tired, cutting corners meant he'd have to go back and do it again. It would have been better to just do a good job in the first place.

It's tempting to think that doing something the easy way is better, but the truth is that most of the time hard work is needed to reach your goals. It is good to be the kind of person who is willing to do hard work. It will make you stronger and teach you perseverance. These are both qualities you will want to have as you get older.

How can you practice being hard working today?

Engaging

But God did listen!
He paid attention to my prayer.

PSALM 66:19 NLT

Campbell knew his parents loved him. He also knew they didn't have as much time to spend with him as they wanted. Life often got busy and with school, soccer games, ballet recitals, and their jobs, things could get out of hand. He loved every moment he spent with his family, but he sometimes wished for more of it.

You are a child of God. He is a perfect Father who is attentive to his children. This means he listens and pays attention to you. He is never too busy for you or too distracted to hear what you need to say. He longs to spend time with you each and every day. If you ever feel ignored or alone, God will always be there to comfort you. Go to him, talk to him, and let him show you how much he loves you.

How can you engage with God today?

Comprehensive

Yes, God is more than ready to overwhelm you with every form of grace, so that you will have more than enough of everything—every moment and in every way. He will make you overflow with abundance in every good thing you do.

2 CORINTHIANS 9:8 TPT

Luciano was learning how to make his grandma's favorite chocolate chip cookies. She sat down with him and carefully explained each step. She didn't skip a single detail. She outlined exactly how much of each ingredient was needed and how to put it all together in the best way. She gave Luciano a comprehensive explanation of how to make the cookies. It would have been ridiculous if she had just told him to throw everything in the bowl and bake it. Instead, she made sure he had a complete understanding of the best way to do it.

Comprehensive means full, complete, and not missing anything. God wants you to have a comprehensive understanding of his grace and love. He wants you to have everything you need in order to get through each day. He is not a stingy God. He doesn't just give you a little bit of what you need. He wants you to be overflowing, not missing anything.

Have you been expecting God to give you barely enough when he wants to give you more?

Approachable

O God in Zion, to you even silence is praise!
You who answers prayer,
all of humanity comes before you with their requests.

PSALM 65:1-2 TPT

Waylon was proud to be his father's son. He loved his dad
more than anyone else. One of his favorite things about his
dad was that he could talk to him about anything. He had
some friends at school who sometimes mentioned being
afraid to talk to their parents. "I'm going to be in so much
trouble when my mom finds out," they would say. Waylon
didn't understand that. He knew no matter what, he could
share about his day with his dad.

Do you have someone in your life who is approachable
like that? Can you imagine then how approachable God is?
You can bring anything to God. There is nothing too big or
too small to talk to God about. There is nothing too scary,
embarrassing, bad, or confusing. No matter what, God wants
to hear from you. He is an approachable God. This means you
don't have to be afraid of him or worried about how he will
react to what you say. He is safe, kind, and always ready with
open arms and a listening ear. No matter how something turns
out, every situation is improved by talking to God about it.

Have you been praying as though God is
approachable or intimidating?

Committed

Commit to the LORD everything you do.
Then he will make your plans succeed.

PROVERBS 16:3 NIRV

Clive sat and watched quietly while his dad tried to fix a leak coming from the ceiling. It had been a day since it started and it seemed like every time he got it fixed, it started leaking again. Clive watched while his dad finally put away his tools and said, "Sometimes you need to know when to call in some help." He picked up his phone and called a plumber.

When you commit something to the Lord it means you are welcoming him into the situation. You are believing that he knows best and if the situation is in his hands, he will handle it. It means you are trusting him to be in control and to work out the details because he is wiser and stronger than you are. It's like trusting an expert to do a job you know is too difficult or complicated for you. When you ask him for help, it shows you know who he is and that he is always there to lead you.

Have you been trying to manage
your life on your own when you could
be committing your days to the Lord?

Enthusiastic

Work with enthusiasm,
as though you were working for the Lord
rather than for people.

EPHESIANS 6:7 NLT

Arden sat in church with his family. They were singing a worship song and he was enjoying telling God how thankful he was for him. As the song ended the worship leader talked about how you can worship God in everything you do, not just with music. Arden had never really thought about that before. He had always thought that worshipping God mostly had to do with singing songs and telling God what you were thankful for. He had never realized that simple, everyday tasks counted as worship.

Everything you do can be done for God. From the moment you wake up until you close your eyes to go to bed, you can honor him with each action, word, and attitude. Each simple task can be done in a way that is worship to God. You can brush your teeth with joy, clean your room with enthusiasm, and get ready for school with a good attitude. Worship doesn't have to be some big act. Even basic, small tasks can be done as though you are doing them for God.

How can you honor God
in simple ways today?

Admire

"The Father loves the Son and shows him everything
he is doing. In fact, the Father will show him how
to do even greater works than healing this man.
Then you will be truly astonished."

JOHN 5:20 NLT

Miguel really looked up to his neighbor. He was a few years
older than him, and he knew everything there was to know
about camping, hiking, and wood carving. He spent most
summer nights in a tent in his backyard and Miguel was
sometimes allowed to join him. He would teach Miguel how
to tie knots or how to start a fire. Miguel wanted to be just
like him. He really admired him.

When you admire someone, you look up to them. You think
highly of them, and you might even copy what they do. It is
good to admire Jesus. His life mirrored who God is and so
when you follow Jesus, you are also following God the Father.
If you ever want to know who God is, just look to Jesus.

What do you admire about Jesus?

Concern

Abandon every display of selfishness.
Possess a greater concern for what matters to
others instead of your own interests.

PHILIPPIANS 2:4 TPT

Maynard and his friends ran outside when the bell rang.
They all rushed toward the ball bin and searched for the best
ones. As the group argued over who got the best soccer ball
or basketball, Maynard watched one boy waiting patiently
to the side. "Don't you want a good one?" he asked. The boy
responded, "Well sure, but I'd rather see someone else be
happy about what they get than argue about it." Maynard was
impressed and thought about how kind it was to think about
what someone else wants over your own wants.

Even though it's not always easy, you are supposed to care
more for what other people need than what you need. This
is not because your needs don't matter. They matter very
much. However, when you care for others, God will take care
of you. There is no one better to take care of what you need
than God. Knowing that God will take care of you means
you can be free to help others instead of yourself.

What is one thing you can do today
to show concern for others?

Made

You will be faithful for all time to come.
You made the earth, and it continues to exist.

PSALM 119:90 NIRV

Juan's grandpa was over at his house trying to help them fix their refrigerator. As he worked to figure out the problem he said, "Man, they really don't make things like they used to." Juan asked what he meant and his grandpa explained that the fridge he used to have lasted him for thirty-five years. He said things used to last a lot longer, and now it was common for an appliance to last less than ten years. Creating something is one thing but creating something to last is a different thing entirely.

God made the earth with just his Words. This in itself is a miracle. Can you imagine speaking something into existence? But not only did God create the earth, but he created everything in it to work together perfectly. He did not just make something temporary; he made it to last. His power is so great that everything he made still exists and works beautifully thousands of years later.

What can you do today to praise God
for all he has made?

Praise

Praise the LORD!
Praise God in his sanctuary;
praise him in his mighty heaven!
Praise him for his mighty works;
praise his unequaled greatness.

PSALM 150:1-2 NLT

Maximo took a deep breath and closed his eyes. He let the worship music that was playing wash over him like a wave. He felt himself relax, and he felt calmer than he had in weeks. The past few weeks of the beginning of the school year had been stressful for him. He'd been trying his best in his classes, and he was tired. He wanted to make his parents proud and hadn't realized how stressed he had been. He'd been so worried about doing his best he hadn't taken any time to rest.

It's not good to focus so much on work that you forget to relax. In the same way, it's not good to be so caught up in trying to follow Jesus so perfectly you forget to praise him! Don't worry yourself with following rules so much that you don't leave any energy for worship. It is good to try to do the right thing but it is also important to enjoy God's presence. Thank him for who he is and praise him for all he has done.

What are three things about God
you can praise him for today?

Refined

The words of the LORD are perfect.
They are like silver made pure in a clay furnace.
They are like gold made pure seven times over.

PSALM 12:6 NIRV

Miles had just recently started reading his Bible regularly. He had read little bits of it in the past, but he had never really sat down and read through it. He was trying to read through Psalms and Proverbs this year. With each chapter he read, Miles learned more and more about who God is. He used to think the Bible was boring, but he was beginning to see just how helpful the Word of God is.

Refined is a word that means something is perfect, precise, and without anything wrong. When silver or gold is refined, it is heated up so any impurities will rise to the surface. Then they are scooped out and the process is continued until what's left is completely perfect. This is how God's Word is. Everything he has said is refined and perfect. You can trust his Word and use it to understand who God is and how you should live your life.

Have you let the perfect and refined Word of God impact your life?

Contribute

When you come together, each of you brings something. You bring a hymn or a teaching or a message from God. You bring a message in another language or explain what was said in that language. Everything must be done to build up the church.

1 CORINTHIANS 14:26 NIRV

Casey loved being part of his church. Some of his favorite Sundays were the ones when they had a church-wide potluck. In the summer, after the service, they would gather in the park across the street and eat lunch together. Every family brought something different. It was a combination of everyone's favorite dishes, and Casey loved trying a little bit of each thing. By the end of the afternoon, everyone had full stomachs and full hearts from enjoying each other's company.

The body of Christ is a lot like a church potluck. Everyone has something to contribute. Without each person bringing something to the table, the meal would be lacking. We have all been given gifts and talents by God. When we each use them in the right way, the church is encouraged and built up. If you went to a potluck and every single person brought the same thing, you would be disappointed. In the same way, we should each be thankful for the gifts God has given us, even if they are different from the person next to you.

Have you ever thought about what gifts God has given you to contribute?

Speak

I will tell everyone about your righteousness.
All day long I will proclaim your saving power,
though I am not skilled with words.

PSALM 71:15 NLT

Pablo knew God had done great things for him. He knew God has saved him and that he was a kind and generous Father. He wanted to share with his friends about who God was, but he was nervous about saying the wrong thing. He didn't want to mess up and he didn't think he knew enough to do a good job.

Go ahead and read today's verse again. Notice what the last line says. The Psalmist says that they will talk about how great God is even though they are not skilled with words. He is saying that even though he might not do a very good job, he will still tell others about how wonderful it is that God has saved him. You don't need to be a talented speaker in order to praise God. You don't have to have all of the right words in order to speak about what God has done.

Have you let a fear of messing up
keep you from sharing about God?

Vital

I have depended on you since I was born.
You have been my help from the day I was born.
I will always praise you.

PSALM 71:6 ICB

Jace loved comic books. Superheroes were his favorite thing to read about, and he was really excited about all of the movies that were coming out lately. He'd spend each bedtime reading about a new hero, learning where he came from, and what his powers were. Each hero had an important history. Without understanding their origin, the superhero didn't make any sense.

You need God. He is the most vital part of your life. Trying to live without him is like trying to understand a comic book without knowing the original story of the superhero. God is your Maker; he is the beginning and the end of your story. He understands you better than anyone. He knew you before you were born, and he knows what each of your days will look like. He is always on your side and is always ready to help you.

Did you know God is a vital part of your life?

Invited

"I was hungry, and you gave me food. I was thirsty, and you gave me something to drink. I was alone and away from home, and you invited me into your house."

MATTHEW 25:35 NCV

Callum was playing soccer with his neighbor on a sunny afternoon. They decided to take a break and so they walked over to a bench nearby. They were both tired and thankful for a chance to rest. When they got to the bench, Callum realized his friend didn't have any water. Without thinking twice, he offered to share what he had even though he was really thirsty and could easily have drunk all of it really quickly. His friend thanked him, and they both felt a little bit refreshed.

The Bible tells us when we are kind to others, it is like we are being kind to Jesus himself. He says when we feed the hungry, it is like we are feeding him. When we comfort the lonely, we are comforting him. Everything we do to make someone else feel loved counts as loving Jesus. When you love others well, you are inviting them to experience God's love. You cannot follow Jesus and say you love him without loving others as well. Treating other people with kindness is a great way to honor God.

How can you show someone the love of God today?

Family

You have received the "Spirit of full acceptance," enfolding
you into the family of God. And you will never feel orphaned,
for as he rises up within us, our spirits join him in saying the
words of tender affection, "Beloved Father!" For the Holy
Spirit makes God's fatherhood real to us as he whispers into
our innermost being, "You are God's beloved child!"

ROMANS 8:15-16 TPT

Family was the most important part of Andreas' life. He had
six siblings, and his grandparents lived just down the street.
He was very close to all of his aunts and uncles, and his
cousins were some of his best friends. They were a big, loud,
happy bunch and his time with them was wonderful. He
couldn't imagine going through life without his family.
They made him feel loved, cared for, and important.

When our earthly families are good, it can give us a glimpse
of what it means to be a part of God's family. You are a part of
God's family. No matter what your own family looks like, you
can be confident you will always belong to the family of God.
When you chose to follow Jesus, you were adopted as a son of
God. This is a title that cannot be taken away from you. It was
given to you by God himself and it cannot be removed. You
will always have a place in his heart, and he will always be
your faithful Father, no matter how old you get.

How does being part of God's family make you feel?

Affirmed

Today the LORD has announced that you are his people. He has said that you are his special treasure. He promised that you would be. He has told you to keep all his commands.

DEUTERONOMY 26:18 NIRV

Thad wandered through the grocery store with his mom. He stopped for a minute to look at something that caught his eye, and when he looked up, he couldn't see his mom anywhere. A few minutes went by, and he still couldn't find her. Suddenly he heard his name being called over the intercom and me made his way up to the front of the store. When he got there, he heard his mom saying, "Yes, that's my son. There he is." Her words told everyone around them she knew who he was.

When you affirm something, you are saying it is true. You are agreeing with what has been said and are saying you are confident in it. It's like your parent saying to someone, "Yes, this is my child." In the same way, God affirms that you are his son. In the Bible he is constantly saying how important you are to him. The Word is one big story about how much God loves his people. If you read it cover to cover, you will see every single page points to how much God loves his creation.

Does God's affirmation give you
confidence in his love for you?

Gratitude

Give thanks for everything to God the Father
in the name of our Lord Jesus Christ.

EPHESIANS 5:20 NLT

After church on Sunday, Cameron started to really pay attention to all of the good things in his life. His Sunday school teacher had asked them each to make a list of twenty things they were thankful for. This seemed like a lot because at first all he could think of were the same old things he always said. Once he started to look beyond those things, he realized he couldn't stop seeing ways in which God had given him good gifts.

If you pay attention, you will never run out of things to be thankful for. Sometimes it can be hard to think of things beyond the basics. It's easy to thank God for your family, your home, and your food. Every good gift is from God. From the sun on your face, to the way your best friend makes you laugh, to the smell of cookies fresh out of the oven. You can thank him for the big things and all of the everyday small things that are a blessing in your life.

What are you thankful for today?

Conduct

A voice came from heaven and said:
"You are my Son and I love you.
I am very pleased with you."

MARK 1:11 ICB

Darcy walked beside his little brother. They were on their way to the park that was across the street from their house. Once they got there, Darcy pushed his brother on the swing and helped him climb the steps to his favorite slide. When they were walking home, an older woman stopped him and said, "You did a great job with your brother. Your parents must be so proud of the way you conduct yourself."

When someone talks about the way you conduct yourself they are talking about the way you act and behave. As a follower of Jesus, you are supposed to conduct yourself in a way which pleases God just like Jesus did. While on earth, Jesus honored God with everything he did. God was very pleased with him, and he announced it proudly when Jesus was baptized. If you are unsure of how to please God, live how Jesus lived. Love others, speak the truth, and talk to God every day.

Does the way you conduct yourself honor God?

Advice

Wise people can also listen and learn;
even they can find good advice in these words.

PROVERBS 1:5 NCV

Cyrus wasn't sure what he should do. He really wanted to go to summer camp but this year it happened to be the same week as both his brother's birthday and the county fair that he loved to go to. He had been thinking about it for a month and he still couldn't decide what he should do. The final day to register for camp had arrived and Cyrus felt frustrated about the whole situation. He sat down at the table with his parents and said, "Well, what would you do if you were me?" They kindly shared their opinions and discussed the issue as a family.

You will never be too wise to ask for help. Whether you are ten, twelve, forty-five, or ninety years old, it is always good to ask for advice. Being willing to ask for help shows you have humility. This means you aren't full of pride, and you know other people have something to offer. When you ask for advice from others it shows that you value their opinions.

Is there something you've been struggling with
that you can ask for advice about?

Devotion

Love flashes like fire,
the brightest kind of flame.
Many waters cannot quench love,
nor can rivers drown it.

SONG OF SOLOMON 8:6-7 NLT

Ronnie loved building models. He and his dad were currently working on a model airplane and Ronnie was really proud of their hard work. Whenever they finished a project, Ronnie would place it on a special shelf in his bedroom. He took extra care to make sure each model was placed securely. He didn't want any of them to fall and break. When he had friends over and they asked to play with the models, Ronnie would explain they weren't toys and suggest something else. He was devoted to making sure his prized possessions stayed safe.

In a similar way, God is devoted to you. He adores you. His love for you is so great that it doesn't have any limits. The Word says that rivers cannot drown it and that it is as bright as a flame. His love for you is greater than anything you will ever experience on earth. He is on your side and is always there to help you and guide you through your days. The Bible is full of examples of how God has proven his devotion to his people.

What is one way God has proven his devotion to you?

Unfailing

Your unfailing love is better than life itself;
how I praise you!
I will praise you as long as I live,
lifting up my hands to you in prayer.
You satisfy me more than the richest feast.
I will praise you with songs of joy.

PSALM 63:3-5 NLT

Marceau's family was moving, and he was nervous about it.
Everything was changing all around him. He'd be leaving the
house and the friends he grew up with, and he felt unsure
about everything. He had so many questions about what the
future would look like in their new home. Even though a
lot of things would be different, he knew God's love for him
would stay the same. He felt comforted knowing the love of
God would never change.

God's love for you is unfailing. He will never give up on you
or leave you alone. His love never ends. He doesn't just love
you sometimes; he loves you all of the time. There is nothing
you can do to change God's love for you. No matter where
you go, God's love is always with you. This can make you feel
safe and secure. No matter what, God will always love you.

When you think about God's unfailing love,
how does it make you feel?

Firm

Teach me to do your will,
for you are my God.
May your gracious Spirit lead me forward
on a firm footing.

PSALM 143:10 NLT

Alexei and his brother raced along the shoreline. Alexei
was scrambling along some big rocks while his brother ran
through the sand. It quickly became obvious that the rocks
were the better choice. He easily moved ahead of his brother
and made it to the tree they had declared was the finish
line. While he waited for him to join him, he watched him
struggle to move quickly over the sand.

When you follow God's will for your life, you will walk on
a firm footing. When your footing is firm, it is like walking
across a rock compared to walking on sinking sand. With a
firm footing, you can easily get where you are going. Even
when things change or you are unsure of what to do, you
can feel confident that God is leading you. He will keep you
steady no matter what kinds of storms life brings.

What can you do if your footing
does not feel secure?

Integrity

The eyes of the LORD are everywhere.
They watch those who are evil and those who are good.

PROVERBS 15:3 NIRV

Dennis loved when his family all got together. He'd play with his cousins, and they would all eat a big meal together. When dessert was announced, Dennis ran into the kitchen before anyone else. He quickly grabbed a plate and claimed the biggest slice as his own. He felt proud of himself for being so quick. But by the time everyone went through the line, there wasn't enough cake to go around, and he felt like he should have shared.

Integrity means doing the right thing even when it seems like no one is watching. Each choice you make counts. It's important to have integrity even in small ways. For example, people might not ever notice you took the biggest piece of cake, but they will notice when you offer it to them first. Little acts of kindness like that can add up to a lifetime of loving others well. Every act of love counts, and God sees it. He will always reward his children for the good things they do.

What is something kind you can do today
that might not get noticed?

NOVEMBER

Because of how I have suffered for Christ, I'm glad that I'm weak. I am glad in hard times. I am glad when people say mean things about me. I am glad when things are difficult. And I am glad when people make me suffer. When I am weak, I am strong.

1 CORINTHIANS 2:10 NIRV

Joy

Those who look to him for help will be radiant with joy;
no shadow of shame will darken their faces.

PSALM 34:5 NLT

Linden really wanted to make dinner for his family. He was
trying hard to do it all on his own, and so far it was working
out alright. He just had a few things left to do and he would
be ready to set the table and serve everyone the meal. He
glanced at the recipe card and came across a word he didn't
understand. He walked confidently up to his mom and asked
her what it meant. He wasn't nervous or frustrated because
he knew she would know what to do. Even though he ran
into a problem, he wasn't stressed because he knew his mom
was on his side.

In the same way, the Word says when you ask God for
help, you will be radiant with joy. This is because someone
who asks God for help knows he is big enough to handle
whatever they are facing. True joy comes from knowing who
God is and having confidence that he will keep all of his
promises to you.

When you ask God for help are you
confident that he will answer you?

Found

"Suppose a woman has ten silver coins and loses one. When she finds it, she will call in her friends and neighbors and say, 'Rejoice with me because I have found my lost coin.' In the same way, there is joy in the presence of God's angels when even one sinner repents."

LUKE 15:8-10 NLT

Dexter looked and looked but he could not find his Swiss Army knife. It had been a gift from his grandfather, and it was really important to him. He wasn't sure what he would do if he couldn't find it. He searched everywhere he could think of and was about to give up when his mom walked into his room. She handed him the knife and said it had accidentally gone through the laundry. He sighed in relief, overjoyed that it wasn't lost after all.

There are billions of people in all of history who have followed Jesus, but God still rejoices over every single one. He never gets bored celebrating each and every salvation. When you chose to love God, you caused great joy in the heavens. Before you knew God, you were lost. Once you put your faith in him, you were found. He rejoices over you just like you would rejoice if you found something you treasured.

Do you feel as though
you are treasured by God?

Pardoned

Evil people should stop being evil.
They should stop thinking bad thoughts.
They should return to the Lord,
and he will have mercy on them.
They should come to our God,
because he will freely forgive them.

ISAIAH 55:7 ICB

Earle struggled to walk into school. His backpack sagged under the weight of his books, and his arms were overflowing. He was trying to balance his science project, a water bottle, the remaining half of his breakfast bagel, and his guitar case. As he fumbled with the door, his best friend ran up. "Give me some of that; you can't carry all of it on your own."

Holding onto the sin in your life is like trying to open a door while you're carrying way too much. There's no need to be weighed down by all of your sin when God is ready and waiting to take it from you. God loves to forgive. He is never ashamed of you, and you don't ever need to be embarrassed to bring your sin to him. He loves to show mercy to his children. There is no sin that is too big for God to forgive. He is always waiting for you to go to him and allow him to help you. He wants to erase your sin and see you walk in freedom.

Have you been holding onto sin
instead of giving it to God to forgive you?

Prepared

Be watchful, and control yourselves completely. In this way,
put your hope in the grace that lies ahead. This grace will be
brought to you when Jesus Christ returns.

1 PETER 1:13 NIRV

Damon really looked up to his dad. When he came home
from work each evening, Damon quickly became his
shadow. He wanted to be wherever he was, doing the same
things. He wanted to spend as much time as possible at his
dad's side. Because he stayed close to him, Damon knew
what he was doing and where he was going.

One day Jesus will come back and make everything right. We
don't know exactly when this will happen, but we can still
be prepared for it. The best way to do that is to stay humble
and aware of your need for God. This means that each day
you realize how much you need him, and you do your best
to stay close to him. If you stay close to Jesus, you will not be
surprised when he comes back.

What can you do today to be closer to Jesus
than you were yesterday?

Relief

Hear my prayer, O LORD;
listen to my plea!
Answer me because you are faithful and righteous.

PSALM 143:1 NLT

Marcus was hiking with his family. They had already done three miles and had another two to do. The view at the top of the ridge had been beautiful but he was so tired. Sweat dripped down his back, and his legs ached. He really regretted packing his backpack so full. After a few more steps he felt like he just couldn't go any further. He looked at his dad and asked if he could please carry his bag for him. His dad took one look at his tired son and easily picked up the bag. He smiled at him and told him to keep going; they were almost done. Without the heavy weight of the bag Marcus found another round of energy, and off they went.

When you go to God with your frustrations or worries, you can experience the same relief you would feel if you handed over a heavy backpack in the middle of a long hike. This is because he is big enough to carry your burdens for you. You can take a deep breath and know that he is in control. He is listening when you speak, and he will always be faithful to answer you.

Have you carried your worries around
when you could be giving them to God?

Fair

If you judge someone else, you have no excuse for it.
When you judge another person, you are judging yourself.
You do the same things you blame others for doing.

ROMANS 2:20 NIRV

Dion sat at the breakfast table with his family. He loved the mornings when they could all eat together. His mom would make something special to eat and they'd get to start the day by being together. When he sat down, he noticed the big pan of fluffy cinnamon rolls. His sister grabbed the serving spoon and immediately went for the largest one. "Hey! I was about to use the spoon!" He yelled. She apologized and gave him the spoon. He immediately grabbed that same large roll. His mom looked at him and reminded him to treat others the way he would want to be treated.

It's only fair to treat others in the same way you want to be treated. It's fair to behave in the same way you would expect others to behave, too. It isn't right to be angry with someone over their actions, then turn around and act the same way yourself. Being fair isn't always easy, and it takes practice to learn how to think about others before you think of yourself.

What is something you can do today
to practice being fair to others?

Sensible

"Teacher, which command in the law is the most important?"
Jesus answered, "'Love the Lord your God with all your heart,
all your soul, and all your mind.' This is the first and most
important command. And the second command is like the
first: 'Love your neighbor as you love yourself.'"

MATTHEW 22:36-39 NCV

Rowan stood in line with his class at the museum. They
were on a field trip that he'd been waiting months for. They'd
been studying dinosaurs in science class and there was a
special exhibit that was only happening for a few weeks.
Rowan couldn't wait to get his hands on the poster of the
giant dinosaur. By the time he got to the front of the line,
there was only one left. He went to grab it, but he noticed the
boy's face behind him. He wanted the poster as well. Rowan
thought for a moment and handed him the poster. The smile
on the other boy's face made it worth it.

If you're unsure of how to love other people well, just think
about how you would like to be treated. It makes sense that if
you wouldn't want others to call you names or leave you out
of an activity, then you shouldn't do that either. When you
treat others the way you want to be treated, it shows them
that God also loves them.

What can you do today to think of someone else
before you think of yourself?

Shelter

In the depths of my heart I truly know
that you, Yahweh, have become my Shield;
You take me and surround me with yourself.
Your glory covers me continually.
You lift high my head.

PSALM 3:3 TPT

Tristan was out riding his bike with his best friend when it started to rain. At first it was just a light drizzle, but it quickly turned into a downpour. They frantically biked over to the pavilion in the park they were passing. Once they were under it, Tristan took a deep breath. They decided to wait it out the rain under the shelter that the pavilion provided. It kept them safe and dry until they were able to get home.

God is your shelter. He's like a pavilion in the middle of a sudden rain. He is the one who keeps you safe and protected from the storms of life. When you are overwhelmed or anxious, you can depend on him to give you a place to rest. He is strong enough to protect you no matter what comes your way. Today, no matter what troubles you might face, remember God is your shelter, and you can rely on him.

When you face troubles,
do you run to God for shelter?

Tender

The LORD is like a father to his children,
tender and compassionate to those who fear him.

PSALM 103:13 NIRV

Felix watched his dad hold his new baby sister in his arms.
He gently rocked her back and forth while she slept. When
she suddenly woke up crying, he hummed a sweet song
and stroked her face until she closed her eyes again. He
was gentle and sweet with her, paying attention to what she
needed. If his dad could be so compassionate with a baby,
Felix imagined God's tenderness must be even greater.

God is tender and compassionate towards his children.
Being compassionate means you think about how other
people feel. What happens to you matters to God. He is
not the kind of God who is only concerned with power
or control. He is tender and loving all of the time.

How have you experienced
God's compassion?

Treasured

People were bringing little children to Jesus. They wanted him to place his hands on them to bless them. But the disciples told them to stop. When Jesus saw this, he was angry. He said to his disciples, "Let the little children come to me. Don't keep them away. God's kingdom belongs to people like them."

MARK 10:13-14 NIV

Gareth loved spending time with his neighbor. No matter when he wandered over there, the older man always had time for him. He would teach Gareth about the car he was restoring or about the plants in his garden. He would tell him stories about when he was younger or offer him a snack and a glass of lemonade. He made Gareth feel important and loved.

You are treasured by God. He values you and says that you are important. He wants you to be near him. He does not have more important things to do, and he is not too busy for you. You are at the very top of his priority list. If someone you know can make you feel loved and cared for, imagine how God feels about you. His love is even more perfect.

How does God's love
make you feel?

Resist

Put on every piece of God's armor so you will be able to resist the enemy in the time of evil. Then after the battle you will still be standing firm.

EPHESIANS 6:13 NLT

Marvin wanted to do the right thing. He knew calling his sister names was wrong but sometimes she just made him so angry. When he was frustrated with her, he had a hard time controlling his emotions. He wanted to speak to her kindly, but he wasn't sure how to resist the temptation to let his anger control him.

To resist means to hold out or to oppose. When you resist sin, it means you are saying no to it. God has given you everything you need to be able to resist sin. When you are tempted to do the wrong thing, you should know you have the power of Christ within you. The same power that raised him from the dead is at work in you, and you can say no to sin just like he did. Ask God to make you strong enough to resist wrong, and he will be faithful to help you.

What is one way you can resist sin today?

Priority

Here is what people who belong to this world do. They try to satisfy what their sinful desires want to do. They long for what their sinful eyes look at. They take pride in what they have and what they do. All of this comes from the world. None of it comes from the Father. The world and its evil desires are passing away. But whoever does what God wants them to do lives forever.

1 JOHN 2:16-17 NIRV

Glenn was really struggling in math class. It wasn't that he couldn't do it, but he didn't want to take the time to practice it. There were so many other things he would rather be doing than studying. After getting a low grade on a test, he finally sat down with his mom to talk about it. She asked him if he had been prioritizing his homework. When he answered that he'd been too busy with soccer, theatre club, and his friends, she replied that if he wanted to get good grades in school, he would have to put his homework first before all of those things.

When something is a priority in your life, it means you put it first. The Bible says we should make God a priority. This means that he is the most important thing in your life and you love him more than anything else. When God is your priority, it is easier to say no to sin. Spend time in prayer, read the Bible, and practice having an attitude of thankfulness.

Have you prioritized your relationship with God?

Provide

"Why do you worry about clothes? Look at the flowers in the field. See how they grow. They don't work or make clothes for themselves. But I tell you that even Solomon with his riches was not dressed as beautifully as one of these flowers. God clothes the grass in the field like that. The grass is living today, but tomorrow it is thrown into the fire to be burned. So you can be even more sure that God will clothe you. Don't have so little faith!"

MATTHEW 6:28-30 ICB

Josef was never worried about what he needed. He knew each day he would have food to eat and a warm bed to sleep in. He would have clothes to wear and a house to live in. He never questioned if he would have what he needed to get through the day. This was because his parents worked hard to make sure everyone was healthy and happy.

If your parents are capable of doing a good job taking care of you, then imagine how much God cares for you. The Bible says to look at the world around you when you are worried about what you have. Notice how everything in nature is taken care of. If God cares for the world around you, he will definitely take care of you. You are much more important to him than flowers and animals.

What can you do if you are worried about having what you need?

Safe

The Sovereign LORD is my strength!
He makes me as surefooted as a deer,
able to tread upon the heights.

HABAKKUK 3:19 NLT

On a beautiful fall day Huey went on a hike with his dad.
They were enjoying the crisp weather and talking about
anything and everything. They made their way down a steep
part of a hill and just as Huey was about to set his foot down
his dad grabbed his shoulder. His foot knocked the rock he
was going to step on, and it tumbled down the hill. His dad's
watchful eye had kept him from tripping or sliding down the
hill with the loose rock.

In the same way, God keeps you steady and safe. He knows
where you can and cannot walk. He knows what each of
your days will look like and how they will impact your life.
When you listen to him, you are putting your trust in a guide
who will never fail you. When you allow him to lead you,
you will always have secure footing.

How can you trust in God's leading today?

Awake

"I say to everyone—be awake at all times."

MARK 13:37 TPT

Jayden walked down the street with his best friend. They were talking about their sleepover next weekend. They were planning on camping out in the backyard, and both of them were really excited about it. His friend said they should go fishing in the morning but Jayden knew his parents would say no to them walking to the lake that early on their own. His friend replied that they wouldn't even know, and they should do it anyway. Jayden thought about going along but decided lying wasn't a good idea. He knew it would only lead to more trouble.

When the Bible talks about staying awake, it's not talking about whether or not you are sleeping. It's talking about being aware of what is going on around you. Life is about more than what you can see with your eyes. There is an epic battle happening all around you. Satan is always trying make God's people slip up and God is always fighting on your behalf. Being awake means noticing opportunities to honor God and also noticing opportunities you should avoid because they will lead to sin.

How can you practice being aware
of what's going on in your life?

Confident

We are confident of all this
because of our great trust in God through Christ.

2 CORINTHIANS 3:4 NLT

Jones had been preparing for his math test for two weeks.
He'd been studying each night before bed and then doing
each assignment with care. He enjoyed math and it was
important to him that he got a good grade on his test. After
all of his hard work, he sat down the morning of the test
feeling confident that he would do well. He knew for sure he
could not have prepared more than he did.

When you are confident in something you are sure of it. It's
the feeling that you know for sure something is right. Just like
you might be confident in your ability to ace a math test, you
can be confident that God will be faithful to you. He will not
leave you to figure out your life alone, but he will always be
near to you helping you through each day. Your confidence
shouldn't be in yourself or in what you can do, but instead
you can rely on how God has saved you. He is the one who
has rescued you and now calls you his son. You can depend
on him and know he is worthy of your trust no matter what.

Where does your confidence lie?

Ambitious

We want each of you to go on with the same hard work all your lives so you will surely get what you hope for.

HEBREWS 6:11 NCV

Lorenzo wanted to be the best at soccer. He practiced at home every day and when he had a team practice, he would try to run the drills with enthusiasm. He was determined to succeed, and so he worked really hard. Even though it wasn't always easy, Lorenzo didn't give up. He put all of his energy into reaching his goal. At the end of the season his coach encouraged him. He told him he was ambitious and hardworking and to keep up the good work.

Someone who is ambitious has a strong desire to succeed. They are determined to do their best at whatever they are tackling. It means not being afraid of hard work and doing whatever it takes to get the job done. This could mean you are ambitious at school, or in sports, or even in the way you love your family and friends. What a wonderful goal, to love your family better than anyone else or to spend as much time with God as you can. Being ambitious is a quality that will take you far in life.

If you are not an ambitious person, how could you practice using that quality?

Unworried

There is no fear in love. Instead, perfect love drives away fear.
That's because fear has to do with being punished.
The one who fears does not have perfect love.
We love because he loved us first.

1 JOHN 4:18-19 NIRV

Lucas really messed up. He and his friends had been tossing a ball outside his house and they had broken a neighbor's car window. His friends had run back to their homes saying their parents would kill them, but Lucas knew he needed to talk to his parents about it. He wasn't excited about the conversation, but he wasn't afraid. They had always made it clear to Lucas that he could talk to them about anything and they had always been true to their word.

If your parents can love you in a way that means you aren't afraid, imagine what God's love can do. There is absolutely no fear in God's love. He is not a God of punishment and heavy-handedness. He is a God of grace, mercy, and encouragement. When you go to him, he will always welcome you. His love is kind, compassionate, and gentle.

Have you ever been afraid of God?
Ask him to show you what his love is really like.

Esteem

You should want a good name
more than you want great riches.
To be highly respected
is better than having silver or gold.

PROVERBS 22:1 NIRV

Kendrick was watching a baseball game at the park with his friend. At the end of the game, an older man walked up to him and said, "Are you Greg Miller's son?" Kendrick looked just like his dad and it made sense that someone would recognize him. The man went on to say he went to college with his dad and after all of these years he still remembered how kind and full of integrity he was. He asked Kendrick to say hi to him and wished him a good day.

When someone esteems you, it means they think highly of you. It means you are respected, and when people think of you they think good things. The Bible says to be esteemed is better than to have a lot of money. It is better to be respected by others because of your character and reputation than to have a lot of money. Strive to be the kind of person others remember because your actions and words remind them of Jesus.

When other people think of you,
what do you think comes to mind?

Willpower

"My food is to be doing the will of him who sent me and bring it to completion." As the crowds emerged from the village, Jesus said to his disciples, "Why would you say, 'The harvest is another four months away'? Look at all the people coming—now is harvest time! For their hearts are like vast fields of ripened grain—ready for a spiritual harvest."

JOHN 4:34-35 TPT

Toby walked with his family through a fall market. He loved the smell of the cider and the way the air felt crisp and refreshing. His parents had given him ten dollars to spend, and he was eagerly looking around for something to buy. He decided he wanted apple donuts and got in line to buy a bucket. As the line moved, his stomach grumbled. Before his turn came up though, he noticed his little brother was crying. He had spent his money on a balloon, and it was flying away. Toby really wanted those donuts; instead, he walked over to the balloon stand, bought a balloon, and smiled as he tied it to his brother's wrist. His desire for donuts didn't go away, but he felt good about doing something nice.

Willpower is the ability to control your actions or emotions. There is wisdom in being able to say no to yourself. You can let your feelings control you, or you can tell yourself no and come up with a better response.

How can you practice using willpower today?

Righteous

May you always be filled with the fruit of your salvation—the righteous character produced in your life by Jesus Christ—for this will bring much glory and praise to God.

PHILIPPIANS 1:11 NLT

Lucien walked through the aisles of the grocery store with his mom. He kept noticing men in army uniforms and he asked his mom what was going on. She said they were giving veterans a big discount on their purchases that day to thank them for their service. Lucien thought about all of the things he would buy if he could have that discount too, but he knew he obviously wasn't qualified for it.

When someone is righteous it means they are in right standing before God. It means they can stand in front of him and be blameless, as though they have done nothing wrong. The Bible says we are righteous because of what Jesus did on the cross. His sacrifice means our sins have been wiped clean and we can be close to God even though we are not perfect enough to be in his presence. Trying to be close to God without Jesus is like trying to get a veterans' discount when you've never served in the army. It's not possible.

How can you thank Jesus for the gift of righteousness?

Journey

In the same way you received Jesus our Lord and Messiah by faith, continue your journey of faith, progressing further into your union with him! Your spiritual roots go deeply into his life as you are continually infused with strength, encouraged in every way. For you are established in the faith you have absorbed and enriched by your devotion to him!

COLOSSIANS 2:6-7 TPT

Marlon had run races for a few years but right now he was training for his first longer one. He wanted to give up, but he knew it would get easier with time. His muscles were tired, and his feet were sore, but he had a goal. He knew he could sprint for a short time, but he was learning how to have endurance. He was learning how to keep running, even when he really wanted to quit.

Your relationship with God is a journey. It's a lot like training for a marathon. There will be times when you want to quit but you need to learn how to have endurance. Following Jesus is a lifetime of choices and opportunities to strengthen your faith. There won't ever be a point when you are finished or done being a Christian. As you get older, your faith will become stronger, and you will gain wisdom but that doesn't mean you ever stop growing.

What can you do today to strengthen yourself for the journey of loving Jesus for your whole life?

Fortress

The LORD is my light and my salvation—
so why should I be afraid?
The LORD is my fortress,
protecting me from danger,
so why should I tremble?

PSALM 27:1 NLT

Nolan loved watching movies about medieval history. He loved watching kings fight over land and defend their castles from invaders. He loved watching knights go on quests or build fortresses to protect the kingdom. They would stand atop thick stone walls and watch for trouble across the land. Even if someone tried to break in, the sturdy gates and the well-built walls would keep the people inside safe.

God is just like that fortress. He surrounds you and keeps you safe. You don't need to be afraid because he himself protects you from danger. The God of the entire universe is on your side. He is strong and capable of handling any trouble that comes your way. When you trust in him, you are placing your trust in the best possible place. With God protecting you, you have no reason to fear.

What is one way you can trust
in God's protection today?

Thankful

No matter what happens, tell God about everything.
Ask and pray, and give thanks to him.
PHILIPPIANS 4:6 NIRV

Kristof felt miserable. He was home from school with a
bad cold, and he was huddled up in his room feeling sorry
for himself. His head hurt, his throat burned when he
swallowed, and he couldn't breathe out of his nose. Usually
skipping school was fun but he would rather be at school
than feel like this. He felt crabby and annoyed. When his
mom came into the room to check on him she could see
how bothered he was. She went and grabbed her computer,
brought him a smoothie, and sat in bed next to him to watch
a movie. Even though he felt gross, Kristof was thankful for
the extra time with his mom.

The Bible says no matter what happens, we should be
thankful. When we are weathering the worst situations there
is always something good, even if it is very small. Learning
how to be thankful in the middle of something difficult is not
an easy thing to do. It's an attitude that takes practice. It would
be much easier to sink into a puddle of sadness, but instead
it's important to be able to see things to be thankful for.

What are three things you can
be thankful for today?

Reconcile

"When you are praying, and you remember that you are angry with another person about something, then forgive him. If you do this, then your Father in heaven will also forgive your sins."

MARK 11:25 ICB

Chester was riding his bike down the sidewalk when he saw one of his neighbors walking towards him. All of a sudden, he felt anger and frustration rise up inside of him. The last time he saw him they had argued and gotten into a fight over something he said. Chester wanted to turn around and go home and pretend he hadn't seen him. It surprised him when the boy walked up and immediately apologized. Chester felt some of his anger shrink away and they talked for a minute about the argument. It surprised him how good it felt to get everything out into the open.

To reconcile means to resolve a problem or to create harmony where there was frustration. When you have a problem with another person, the best way to fix it is to talk to them and seek forgiveness. Don't hold your anger inside where it will grow into bitterness. Admit when you are wrong and ask for forgiveness. If someone else has hurt you, ask God to help you manage the situation. He will heal your heart and help you if you need to talk to that person.

Is there someone in your life you should reconcile with?

Credit

Remember the LORD in all you do,
and he will give you success.

PROVERBS 3:6 NCV

Travis had some friends over after school one day. When they got to his house, they all ran to the back yard. When they saw his newly built tree house, they all talked about how great it was. Each boy commented on his favorite part and Travis felt really proud of it. He wanted to say he had built it himself but that wasn't exactly true. He had helped, but his dad had done most of the work. It wouldn't be fair to pretend he had done it alone.

When you give someone credit for something it means you are acknowledging the effort they gave. It means you aren't pretending you did something on your own when you actually had help. It is wrong to take ownership for something you didn't do. In all that we do, we are supposed to give credit to God. This means remembering that he is our strength and the reason for any of our success. He is the one helping you through each day, and he is the one who is in control of your life.

What is something you can
give credit to God for today?

Helped

Because the Sovereign LORD helps me,
I will not be disgraced.
Therefore, I have set my face like a stone,
determined to do his will.
And I know that I will not be put to shame.

ISAIAH 50:7 NLT

Lennox was working on a project in art class. They were supposed to paint a portrait of their favorite person. They had started their paintings in class but were told they would need to finish them on their own time at home. Lennox was confident his picture would turn out okay because his grandpa was a professional artist. He planned on asking him for help and he knew his grandpa would give him some good pointers. He wasn't worried about doing the project because he believed in his grandpa's skill and talent.

If you needed to do a painting and your grandfather was a professional, you would ask him for help. If you needed to fix your bike and your dad was a mechanic, you would ask him for help. In the same way, you can be confident that God will help you when you need it. No matter what you are going through, God is able to help you. He has all of the right skills and is always eager to help his children. You can be confident in God.

When you need help,
do you go to God?

Victorious

I trust in your love.
My heart is happy because you saved me.
I sing to the LORD
because he has taken care of me.

PSALM 13:5-6 NCV

Winning is a great feeling. It's exciting to be the first to cross
the finish line, score the most points, or get a perfect grade.
You might feel happy, thankful, and relieved all at the same
time. When you win something, that good feeling doesn't
just go away as soon as you've won. It stays with you for
days, weeks or even years. You will always remember those
times because of the pride you feel at doing such a good job.

You are victorious because of God's love. You will win for all
of eternity because of what Jesus has done for you. No matter
what is going on in your life, you can always rejoice because of
how God has taken care of you. The victory you have because
of Jesus is something that can never be taken away from you.

How do you feel knowing you will win forever?

Truthful

"The Spirit of truth. The world cannot accept him,
because it does not see him or know him.
But you know him, because he lives with you
and he will be in you."

JOHN 14:17 NCV

Adrian sat next to his friend at the lunch table. The other boy could not stop talking about his older brother. He clearly loved him a lot and no matter what Adrian said, the boy somehow brought the conversation back to his brother. He talked about how smart he was, how cool he was, and how talented he was. He only had kind and wonderful things to say about him. From what the boy said, Adrian assumed his brother must be really awesome.

This is kind of how the Holy Spirit works. No matter what, he will always remind you about the goodness of God. One of the reasons we have the Holy Spirit is help us find the truth. If you let him, the Holy Spirit will always point you to what is good and right. He reminds you of what the Bible says, and he helps you remember what God has said in the past. He will remind you of what God has already done for you and all the ways he has been faithful.

Did you know you can rely on the Holy Spirit
to help you know what is true?

Unselfish

"I came down from heaven to do what God wants me to do.
I did not come to do what I want to do."

JOHN 6:38 ICB

Nixon wanted to help his mom in the garden but he wasn't exactly sure what to do. He was worried he would ruin her hard work by pulling out a plant that he thought was a weed. He went outside with her and watched her carefully. He asked her questions and he listened to her answers. When she did something, he copied her.

Jesus did not come to earth with his own plans. He did only what his Father asked him to do. He did not think about what he wanted to do or how he wanted to act. He was never selfish. He only thought about what God wanted. Just like you might learn how to tend a garden from your mom, you can learn about who God is by following Jesus. As you follow Jesus, you'll learn from his example of how to be unselfish. It takes practice to learn how to listen to God. The more time you spend with him, learning about who he is, the more you'll know what he sounds like and how to hear what he says to you.

Are you more worried about
your own plans or God's plans?

DECEMBER

Look to the LORD
and to his strength.
Always look to him.

1 CHRONICLES 16:11 NIRV

Wait

Be still in the presence of the LORD,
and wait patiently for him to act.
Don't worry about evil people
who prosper or fret about their wicked schemes.

PSALM 37:7 NLT

Emil was tired of waiting. Christmas was still a month away and he couldn't stand the anticipation. It was his favorite time of the year. He loved how his house felt joyful and full of peace. He loved celebrating Jesus' birth, and he loved the time he got to spend with his family. He enjoyed daydreaming about what presents might be under the tree and what goodies might be in his stocking. The worst part was the waiting.

Waiting is a normal part of life. You can't avoid it. Sometimes trusting God means you need to wait. We often want God to fix a problem as soon as we ask for an answer but that isn't always how he does things. He is wiser than we are, and his timing is perfect. He does everything at just the right time. If you get tired of waiting, you can still trust there is a good reason for it.

How can you practice having patience if
there something you are waiting for right now?

New

This means that anyone who belongs to Christ has become a new person. The old life is gone; a new life has begun!

2 CORINTHIANS 5:17 NLT

Wyatt was working on a painting for art class. He was carefully trying to get the detail right on a tree branch when the paint bottle tipped over and spilled over his canvas. He felt shocked and frustrated. With a big sigh, he put the piece in the trash and pulled out a fresh canvas. It was new and clean, and he could paint whatever he wanted. There were endless opportunities to create on a fresh page.

Just like a blank canvas is ready to become a masterpiece, you are clean and new because of what Jesus has done for you. When you chose to follow Jesus, you were made new. At that moment, a miracle happened. The old you is gone and you have a new life now. The mistakes you made in the past have been covered by the blood of Jesus, and you are free. And after that, each time you go to Jesus for forgiveness, you are made new again. This is the good news of the gospel!

Have you been holding on to past mistakes even though Jesus says you are new and free?

Favorite

In Christ, there is no difference between Jew and Greek,
slave and free person, male and female.
You are all the same in Christ Jesus.

GALATIANS 3:28 NCV

Percy and his family were about to leave on a vacation. He slung his backpack over his shoulder, grabbed a stack of books and headed towards the car. When his mom saw him, she exclaimed, "Percy, we do not have room for all of those books in our luggage. You're going to have to pick one or two." Percy felt frustrated. They were all his favorites, and he couldn't possibly only bring one or two.

We all have favorites. We have our favorite people, our favorite foods, and our favorite places. God does not have favorites. Isn't that incredible? Imagine a love so perfect and pure that everyone gets to experience it equally and without limit. There have been billions and billions of people on the planet, and God loves each of them in exactly the same way. This kind of love is hard for us to understand. The only response we can have to a love this great is to be thankful and to praise him for how wonderful he is.

Do you know you are God's favorite creation?

Courage

"Do not be afraid," he said. "You are highly respected.
May peace be with you! Be strong now. Be strong."
When he spoke to me, I became stronger.
I said, "Speak, my master. You have given me strength."

DANIEL 10:19 NIRV

Renzo was driving home with his dad. It was snowing really hard, and the roads were more and more icy as time went by. The first time Renzo drove in a snowstorm he was nervous and stressed out about getting into a car accident. This time though, he felt okay. He didn't feel brave because he could keep the car steady, but because he knew his dad was a confident and capable driver. He'd driven in storms before, and Renzo knew they would be okay.

When the Bible tells you to be strong and to have courage, it's not because you are capable of being brave all on your own. God isn't telling you to trust in yourself or to rely on your own skills. He is telling you to have courage because he is on your side, and you can rely fully on him. You don't need to be afraid, not because you can handle it, but because God can handle it. You don't have to muster up courage; you just have to trust God.

When you are afraid, did you know
you can be brave because of who God is?

Meek

"When you give to someone in need, don't do as the hypocrites do—blowing trumpets in the synagogues and streets to call attention to their acts of charity! I tell you the truth, they have received all the reward they will ever get."

MATTHEW 6:2 NLT

Ford had started to notice that his mom was always doing kind things for others. He hadn't really paid attention before but the more he thought about it, the more he saw that she was constantly helping whomever she could. She would pay for someone's groceries, or make crying babies smile, or bring flowers to a friend. She loved everyone she came across, but he never heard her talk about it. She didn't brag or make a big deal out of the things she did.

Someone who is meek knows they are powerful but they don't boast about it or lord it over others. To be meek means that even though you could, you choose not to share all of the good things you've done. Instead of looking for people to praise you, you let God reward your actions in his timing. It's not always easy to be meek, but it is worth it.

How can you practice being meek today?

Perseverance

Be patient until the Lord comes. See how the farmer waits
for the land to produce its rich crop. See how patient the
farmer is for the fall and spring rains.

JAMES 5:7 NIRV

Roy hated waiting. His parents told him when he turned
twelve he could move into the guest room, and for the first
time ever he'd have a bedroom all to himself. Part of the
deal was that he needed to show them he could do his part
in keeping his current room tidy before he was given the
new space. He wanted to quit because he was tired of being
diligent, but he knew if he gave up, he wouldn't get the reward.

Perseverance is the ability to keep going even when
something is difficult. When you want to quit but you don't,
you are persevering. Sometimes following Jesus is hard, and
you might want to give up. In those moments, it is important
to be patient and to remember God always keeps his
promises even if it takes time.

Is there something you are waiting for right now?
How can you patiently persevere?

Healing

The man jumped up and went home! Fear swept through the crowd as they saw this happen. And they praised God for giving humans such authority.

MATTHEW 9:7-8 NLT

Taylor had never been so excited. His little brother had been really sick over the past few months, and they'd just been given the news that he was getting better. They had been praying for a miracle, and it seemed like this was it. God had heard them! He had answered their prayers. Taylor felt like jumping and shouting. He couldn't believe God had healed his brother.

God does miracles, big and small, to give us a little taste of what eternity will be like. We don't know what it looks like to live in a perfect place but one day we will know. Right now, when we see someone be miraculously healed, we are in awe. When Jesus comes back, those types of miracles will be completely normal. He will heal everything that is broken, sick, or not right.

Have you ever seen a miracle happen?

Protection

The Lord sees all we do;
he watches over his friends day and night.
His godly ones receive the answers they seek
whenever they cry out to him.

PSALM 34:15 TPT

Beau was watching his younger sister while his mom got ready for the day. She was almost two years old and could be a handful. He steered her away from the stairs more times than he could count. He pulled things out of her mouth, and he made sure she didn't get ahold of anything unsafe. She was curious and often didn't understand what was safe and what wasn't.

God is always protecting you. He is aware of you, and he pays attention to all of your days. He is the one who keeps you safe even when you don't know it. He watches over you and takes care of what you need. Just like when someone keeps a close eye on a small child, God keeps a close eye on you and protects you when you don't even know you need it.

Can you look back and see how God
has kept you safe in the past?

Compassion

If anyone sees a fellow believer in need and has the means to help him, yet shows no pity and closes his heart against him, how is it even possible that God's love lives in him?

1 JOHN 3:17 TPT

Thor sat in the cafeteria at lunchtime. He hadn't realized he'd forgotten his lunch until it was too late to call his mom for help. He didn't have any spare change for a snack and so he sat and wondered what he should do. While he was thinking, his friend sat down beside him and offered him a sandwich. "I always eat two sandwiches," he said, "but I don't need to today." Thor was thankful for his generosity. That small act of kindness made him feel loved and taken care of.

You should always help others when you are able to. The older you get, the more you might notice that not everyone has the same life. Some people have good jobs while others don't. Some people have nice homes and lots of food while others struggle to get what they need. If you can share what you have, you should, especially if you have more than you need. When you show compassion to others, you teach them about the generous love of God.

What can you do today to show someone else the generous love of God?

Dedicated

"The Lord searches all the earth for people who
have given themselves completely to him.
He wants to make them strong."

2 CHRONICLES 16:9 ICB

Easton loved playing basketball. When he wasn't shooting
baskets, he was thinking about it. When he woke up in the
morning, the first thing he saw were the posters around his
room of his favorite NBA players. Basketball season was his
absolute favorite time of the year. He couldn't wait for the
practices, the drills, and the games. His dream was to play
professionally, and he wanted to do everything he could to
make that dream a reality. He was devoted to the game.

When you dedicate yourself to someone or something, you
are promising to be faithful. This means you promise to be
loyal and devoted. God asks you to be devoted to him. He
wants you to give him your whole heart. He doesn't just want
people who believe in him or think it's a good idea to follow
him. He wants you to love him with everything you have.

Would you say you are devoted to God?

Assurance

Let us look only to Jesus, the One who began our faith and
who makes it perfect. He suffered death on the cross.
But he accepted the shame as if it were nothing because
of the joy that God put before him. And now he is sitting
at the right side of God's throne.

HEBREWS 12:2 NCV

Branson and his dad were watching a football game on a
Sunday afternoon. The score was close, and they really didn't
know who was going to win. Branson was really hoping his
team would win because if they did, his dad said he would
take him out for ice cream. If his dad's team won, Branson
had to shovel the snow off the sidewalk. They had made the
friendly bet when game started. Branson had a lot of faith in
his team.

When you put your faith in something, you are saying you
believe in it. You are saying that you trust it will work out
the way you want it to. Sometimes we put our faith in the
wrong thing. We gamble or take a chance on something, and
it doesn't work out. Putting your faith in Jesus is a sure thing.
You are guaranteed to win when you put your trust in him.
It's never a gamble, and he will be victorious.

Where have you placed your faith?

Winning

Thank God! He gives us victory over sin and death through our Lord Jesus Christ.

1 CORINTHIANS 15:57 NLT

Tomas knew it was wrong to lie but he couldn't seem to stop doing it. He especially loved to exaggerate and tell white lies when he was sharing stories with his friends. He wasn't sure how it started, but now nearly everything he said to them was full of small lies that made him look cooler, funnier, or stronger. He wanted to tell the truth, but he wasn't sure he could stop. He knew lying was a sin but he felt stuck in the pattern he had developed.

God has given you victory over sin! This means you don't have to sin over and over again. You can be free from doing the things you don't want to do. You are not trapped or stuck doing the wrong thing. The same power that brought Jesus back from the dead is available to you. You can overcome sin because of what Jesus did. You can win instead of feeling like sin has control over you. The truth is, God has defeated sin and it can't control you anymore as long as you are depending on God.

Have you ever felt stuck in sin?

Vulnerable

Nothing in all creation is hidden from God.
Everything is naked and exposed before his eyes,
and he is the one to whom we are accountable.

HEBREWS 4:13 NLT

Stuart laughed at his younger sister. She walked into the
kitchen with chocolate smeared all over her hands and face.
When his mom asked her if she had snuck a chocolate chip
cookie, she insisted she had not. She refused to admit that she
had eaten the cookie, even though the evidence was all over
her face. She truly believed she could hide what she had done,
even though it was so obvious to everyone else in the room.

God sees everything. We are vulnerable before him. This means
that nothing can be hidden from him. He knows your thoughts
and the deepest parts of your heart. You can't have secrets from
God. There is no reason to hide anything from him because
he always knows the truth. Hiding something from God is like
a toddler trying to convince her mom she didn't eat a cookie
when there's chocolate on her face. This should make you feel
free and cared for. God knows the best and worst parts of who
you are, and he loves you no matter what.

Have you ever tried to hide the truth from God?

Unwavering

Run as fast as you can from all the ambitions and lusts of youth; and chase after all that is pure. Whatever builds up your faith and deepens your love must become your holy pursuit. And live in peace with all those who worship our Lord Jesus with pure hearts.

2 TIMOTHY 2:22 TPT

Baron was trying to save up his money for a hover board. His best friend had one, and he couldn't wait until they could play together. He put all of his money in a jar in his room and refused to spend it on anything else. He was unwavering in his pursuit of what he wanted. He did extra chores, and he mowed his neighbor's lawn. He was sometimes tempted to spend the money he had on something smaller, but he kept his focus and was determined to reach his goal.

An unwavering pursuit of God is a way of saying that you have a goal, and you don't get distracted from it. Give as much attention as you can to living a life that honors God. This doesn't mean you need to constantly be reading your Bible or praying every minute of the day. You can honor God by being kind to others, by being thankful, by enjoying his creation, and by being confident in who he made you to be.

Is your pursuit of God unwavering?

Connected

"I am the sprouting vine and you're my branches.
As you live in union with me as your source,
fruitfulness will stream from within you—
but when you live separated from me you are powerless."

JOHN 15:5 TPT

Zander loved helping his dad in the yard. This weekend they
were trimming trees. His dad would remove the branches
he didn't want, and Zander would drag them over to a pile
they had started. In the spring the trees would blossom again
and sprout leaves but Zander knew none of the branches in
the pile would. They would use them to make campfires, but
they would never provide shade for their yard again.

When you spend time with Jesus, you are like a branch that
is connected to the rest of the tree. Everything you need
comes from staying connected. When you don't stay close to
Jesus you will find you cannot live the way you were meant
to live. Stay close to him by praying, reading the Word, and
thinking about what you love about him.

What can you do today to stay connected to Jesus?

Benefit

All of this is for your benefit. And as God's grace reaches
more and more people, there will be great thanksgiving,
and God will receive more and more glory.

2 CORINTHIANS 4:15 NLT

Frankie had decided when he was really little that he wanted
to follow Jesus. He was thankful for all God had done for
him but lately he was starting to feel like there were too many
rules. He was overwhelmed by the feeling he just wasn't good
enough. He was worried about disappointing God.

Everything God has done is to benefit you. Sometimes you
might feel like being a Christian is hard or that there are
too many rules. The truth is if you are focused on what you
cannot do, you are missing the point. God gave his one and
only Son so we could live forever. He gave what is most
precious to him so we could have our sins wiped away. He
has done great and wonderful things for you. His grace is
enough for you. If you are ever worried that you aren't good
enough, remember God's grace is yours and he is what
makes you good.

Have you ever felt like you aren't good enough?

Belief

All the people were amazed and said,
"Perhaps this man is the Son of David!"

MATTHEW 12:23 NCV

Quentin knew deep in his heart that Jesus was the Son of God. He trusted that he was raised from the dead, and he believed he was the only one who could forgive his sins. He knew all of this is true but sometimes he felt like his faith wasn't very strong. He wanted to be like the great men of the faith he learned about from his parents and in church. He wanted to do great things for God!

Can you imagine living in the time when Jesus walked the earth? If you saw him perform miracles in person, do you think you would have believed who he was? The Bible says you will be even more blessed than those people because you believe in Jesus without ever seeing him face-to-face. You trust that he is the Son of God and he rose from the dead even though you weren't there to see it. You have great faith! Even on days when you don't feel like it, your faith in God makes him very proud.

Did you know your faith makes God proud?

Grant

God has proved his love by giving us his greatest treasure, the gift of his Son. And since God freely offered him up as the sacrifice for us all, he certainly won't withhold from us anything else he has to give.

ROMANS 8:32 TPT

Archer was playing on the floor with his younger brother. The little boy lost interest in what he was doing and so Archer gave him his slingshot to play with. It was his favorite possession, but he knew his brother would enjoy it. His brother was more important to him than the slingshot and he knew that sharing it would bring him joy. His love for his brother caused him to be generous with all he had.

In the same way, when God gave us Jesus, he gave us the very best he had to offer. He gave you Jesus because of his great love for you. He freely granted us the most valuable thing he had. There might be times in your life when you feel like God isn't giving you what you want. If that happens, it's important to remember he has done nothing but the best for you. There will never be a time when God simply stops doing what is best for you.

How can you share God's generous love with someone today?

Compare

"There is no one holy like the Lord.
There is no God but you.
There is no Rock like our God."

1 SAMUEL 2:2 ICB

Brent was working on a comparison project for school.
He was supposed to pick two methods of transportation
and decide which one was better. He chose his items and
carefully began thinking about all of the qualities of each.
He made a list of pros and cons and after he made his final
decision, he wrote out his observations on the worksheet his
teacher had given him.

When you compare two things, it means you are trying
to decide which one is better. In order to make a good
comparison, you need to know as much as you can about
what you are comparing. Many people will claim there are
other gods, but the truth is none of them compare to the one
true God we serve. Our God is good all the time. He is full
of justice and mercy. He is always perfect, always kind, and
always wise. If you didn't know anything about God, you
wouldn't be able to make the right comparison. It's important
to learn as much as you can about him because then you will
be confident about who he is.

What is your favorite characteristic of God?

Recall

I will praise the Lord.
I won't forget anything he does for me.

PSALM 103:2 TPT

Ian walked the familiar trails in the woods behind his house. Now that it was winter, it was harder to tell exactly where he had walked before. When he felt a bit unsure of his path, he looked around and saw a specific tree. It helped him remember which way he was going. Next, he noticed a large rock, then a piece of a broken fence. If he paid attention, there were landmarks everywhere reminding him which way to go.

In the same way, remembering God's faithfulness can act like a roadmap for you. If you ever feel like you don't know how to praise God, try and remember all of the good things he has done for you. If you feel stuck when it comes to worship or prayer, take some time to think about what he has done in the past. When you recall what he has done for you, it can spark thankfulness in your heart. It is good to expect new things from God, but it is also good to remember how faithful he has already been.

What are three things that God has done for you in the past which remind you of his goodness?

Chosen

Give praise to the God and Father of our Lord Jesus Christ.
He has blessed us with every spiritual blessing. Those
blessings come from the heavenly world. They belong to
us because we belong to Christ. God chose us to belong to
Christ before the world was created. He chose us to be holy
and without blame in his eyes. He loved us.

EPHESIANS 1:3-4 NIRV

Derek was so excited to plan his birthday party. He was
writing down ideas on a sheet of paper and was currently
thinking about who he should invite. His mom had said he
could have ten friends over and he wanted to make the right
choices. He carefully thought about each name he added to
the list. None of them were added by mistake or by accident.
Each friend was chosen because he wanted to spend his
special day with them.

God chose you to be his son. You are not an accident or a
mistake. You are part of his family because he wants you to
be. The Creator of the entire universe knows you better than
anyone else, and he has decided you are worth his attention.
Sometimes life can be hard, and days can be difficult. In those
times, remember how valuable God says you are. Even on your
worst day, you are still chosen by him.

How does knowing you are
chosen by God make you feel?

Goal

Our only goal is to please God
whether we live here or there.

2 CORINTHIANS 5:9 NCV

Kees loved to do lists. He liked to be organized and to work towards reaching a goal. He enjoyed being able to say he did what he said he would do. It didn't matter if he were working towards a good grade in science, a winning soccer game, keeping his room clean, or getting chores done early so he could play video games. No matter what the task was, Kees loved the feeling of accomplishment that came with getting something done.

It's great to have goals. Getting things done is important. No matter what is on your to-do list, remember the most important goal you will ever have is to please God. Everything you do can be an act of worshipping him. Seek to follow Jesus' example and strive to glorify God in all you do.

What can you do when you've made other goals
more important than following Jesus?

Calm

Fully awake, he rebuked the storm and shouted to the sea,
"Hush! Be still!" All at once the wind stopped howling and
the water became perfectly calm.

MARK 4:39 TPT

Nico looked out the window. They were in the middle of
a snowstorm and he watched as the trees bent in the wind
while the snow swirled around furiously. Mounds of it piled
up, and he knew they would be staying home the next day. It
was the worst winter storm they'd had in a long time. Nico
thought about Jesus calming the storm, and he couldn't
imagine all of the chaos outside stopping after he spoke a
single word.

God is big enough that even the stormy sea will listen when
he speaks. If he can calm the raging waves, then he can
calm your heart when you are overwhelmed. Sometimes
when you feel anxious it might seem like nothing is going
your way or that your emotions are out of control. In those
moments, ask God for help. Give him your frustrations, and
he will give you peace.

What is something you can do when you are anxious
in order to turn your attention to God?

Simple

"Those who are humble are happy.
The earth will belong to them."

MATTHEW 5:5 ICB

Dax had been waiting for Christmas all year. His grandma always gave the best gifts, and this year was no exception. She got him the skateboard he had been asking for and even gave it to him early so he could get more use out of it. He loved it for a while. By the time Christmas Day rolled around, Dax had already stopped skateboarding as much and was wondering what else he would get. The skateboard that he had wanted so badly sat unused in the corner of his room.

The Bible says the humble are happy because they know that true happiness doesn't come from themselves or from things. If you spend your life searching for the next thing to make you happy, you will always need more. Before long, the new and exciting toy won't be new or exciting anymore. You'll move on and decide you want something better to make you happy. When you live like that, you'll always be searching for the next thing. Instead, learn how to be content with what you have. Letting simple things bring you happiness will give you joy for the rest of your life.

Do you feel happy with what you have
or are you always looking for more?

Wonderful

There were shepherds living out in the fields nearby. It was night, and they were taking care of their sheep. An angel of the Lord appeared to them. And the glory of the Lord shone around them. They were terrified. But the angel said to them, "Do not be afraid. I bring you good news. It will bring great joy for all the people. Today in the town of David a Savior has been born to you. He is the Messiah, the Lord."

LUKE 2:8-11 NIRV

Lance held his baby sister in his arms. She had just been born a month ago and this was her first Christmas. She was asleep and he watched her tiny fingers curl around his thumb. Watching his mom take care of her made Lance realize how much work babies are. They need you to do everything for them. He felt amazed that Jesus chose to come to earth as a baby who would need so much help when he could have used his great power in any way he wanted.

Jesus could have come to earth in a parade of glory. He could have made a huge scene and declared that he was the rightful King. Instead, he came humbly as a baby. He walked around in a body just like yours, and he felt happy and sad just like you do. He is the Savior of the world and he chose to be just like us. Jesus is a wonderful gift.

If Jesus chose to be weak like a baby, what does that tell you about him?

Breathtaking

How could I be silent when it's time to praise you?
Now my heart sings out, bursting with joy—
a bliss inside that keeps me singing,
"I can never thank you enough!"

PSALM 30:12 TPT

Tristan sat at the window and looked outside. He and his family were at his grandparents' farm for Christmas. It was one of Tristan's favorite places in the entire world. He watched the snow fall over the rolling hills and he felt happy to be there. The whole farm was sparkling and white. It was gorgeous. Tristan thanked God for such a beautiful picture and went to play with his cousins.

Picture the most beautiful thing you've ever seen. Maybe it's a beautiful view over the ocean, or a field full of wildflowers. God is breathtaking. The most glorious sunset or the most rugged mountain range cannot compare to him. After all, he is the one who dreamed up and created all of those things. If creation is so incredible, imagine how breathtaking the Creator is. We will never fully understand his beauty until we see him face-to-face but for now, we can look at all he has made and know that it reflects who he is.

What part of creation are you most thankful for?

Inside

The LORD said to Samuel, "Don't look at how handsome
Eliab is or how tall he is, because I have not chosen him.
God does not see the same way people see. People look at the
outside of a person, but the LORD looks at the heart."

1 SAMUEL 16:7 NCV

There was a group of kids at Denver's school whom everyone
labeled, "the cool kids." Denver really wanted to be a part of
that group, but he wasn't sure they would want him there. He
didn't really look like them or act like them. Mostly, Denver
just wanted to fit in. He couldn't change what he looked like,
but maybe if he changed how he acted, they'd invite him into
their group.

We live in a world that focuses a lot on what things look
like. This is completely different from how things work in
the kingdom of God. God doesn't care what someone looks
like on the outside. He is more concerned about their hearts.
He sees everything that is going on inside of you. You can't
pretend anything, nor can you fool God. He knows what
you think and feel even if you've never told anyone before.
He sees everything, and he is not ashamed of you. He knows
everything about you, and he will love you forever.

What can you do when you are more concerned
about how you look and act than you are
about the motivations of your heart?

Exalted

In that glorious day, you will say to one another, "Give thanks to the Lord and ask him for more! Tell the world about all that he does! Let them know how magnificent he is!" Sing praises to the Lord, for he has done marvelous wonders, and let his fame be known throughout the earth!

ISAIAH 12:4-5 TPT

Holden wanted to talk about God with his friends, but he wasn't sure how. It made him nervous, and he wasn't sure what they would think of him. He felt like he needed to say just the right thing. He was worried that he wouldn't explain things right or he'd share something incorrectly from the Bible.

The world exalts people for the things they do but we called to exalt God. One way you can do that is to tell other people about him. Tell them what he has done for you and how he has changed your life. Talk about how good he is and what your favorite things about him are. Exalting God doesn't have to be complicated. It's good to share Scripture but it's also good to share what God has done for you personally.

How does the idea of sharing God
with others make you feel?

Fascinating

Be in awe before his majesty.
Be in awe before such power and might!
Come worship wonderful Yahweh,
arrayed in all his splendor,
bowing in worship as he appears in the beauty of holiness.
Give him the honor due his name.

PSALM 29:2 TPT

Dante stared wide-eyed at the night sky. He had never seen so many stars in his entire life. It was incredible. The sky was covered with millions of shining lights that were brighter and more vivid than anything he'd ever seen. He couldn't help but think about how lucky he was to see them. If God made a night sky like that, then he must be truly wonderful and full of splendor.

When creation takes your breath away, remember who the Creator is. When you are in awe of something he has made, it is the same thing as being in awe of him. Let creation point you to how wonderful he is. Worship him for all he has done and all he has made. Thank him for who he is and praise him for how much he loves you. If you spend your life being fascinated with God, you'll have spent your time well.

Have you ever been fascinated
with something God made?

Model

Do what is good. Set an example for them in everything.
When you teach, be honest and serious. No one can
question the truth. So teach what is true. Then those
who oppose you will be ashamed. That's because
they will have nothing bad to say about us.

TITUS 2:7-8 NIRV

Dimitri loved his Uncle Tim. He was easy to talk to, and he
always had something encouraging to say. He made Dimitri
feel loved and important. He taught him how to fish, how to
find the best comics at the bookstore, and how to memorize
Scripture. Dimitri was thankful for the example his uncle
provided him. He learned a lot about how to follow Jesus
from him.

Do you have someone in your life who models the love of
Jesus and teaches you about who God is? It is important to
have people who are older and wiser than you to look up to.
No matter how old you are, you will never be too old to learn
from others. Following the example of someone who loves
the Lord and knows the Word is one of the best ways to live a
life that honors God. He made us to need each other, and one
of the reasons is so we can teach each other about who he is.

Who do you look to for encouragement in your faith?

Belong

You are a chosen people, royal priests, a holy nation,
a people for God's own possession. You were chosen
to tell about the wonderful acts of God, who called you
out of darkness into his wonderful light.

1 PETER 2:9 NCV

Spencer really wanted to be on the basketball team.
He'd worked hard and was excited about how much he'd
improved. So, when he twisted his ankle during tryouts, he
was devastated. When he talked to his mom about it, she
explained that he could try out again next year, but in the
meantime, he was an important part of many other teams.
He was a valuable player in his family, in his classroom, and
in the body of Christ.

You probably belong to more than one group. You belong
to your family, to your group of friends, to your class, and
to your sports team. All of these are groups you belong to.
You are a part of them. You contribute to them, and you
are needed. More importantly than any of those things,
you belong to body of Christ. You are part of a much larger
family. You are chosen by God to be in his family. You are
needed and valued. You have a unique role to play, and the
world wouldn't be the same without you.

How does it feel knowing that you belong to God?